THE
UNDERGROUND
RAILROAD
IN OHIO

KATHY SCHULZ

THE
History
PRESS

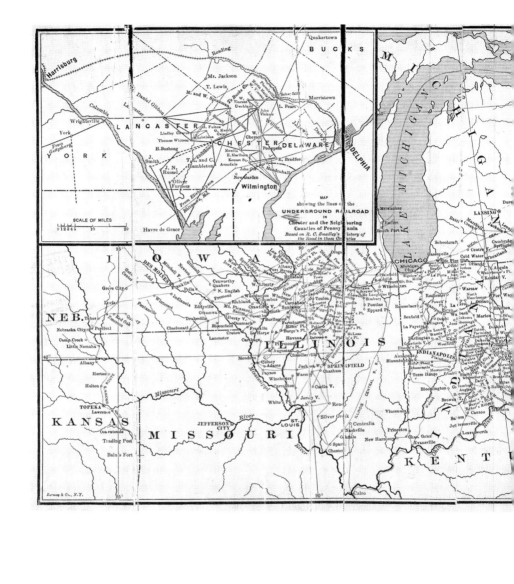

MAP
showing the lines of the
UNDERGROUND RAILROAD
IN
Chester and the Neighboring
Counties of Pennsylvania
Based on R. C. Smedley's History of
the Road in these Counties

SCALE OF MILES
0 1 2 3 4 5   10   20

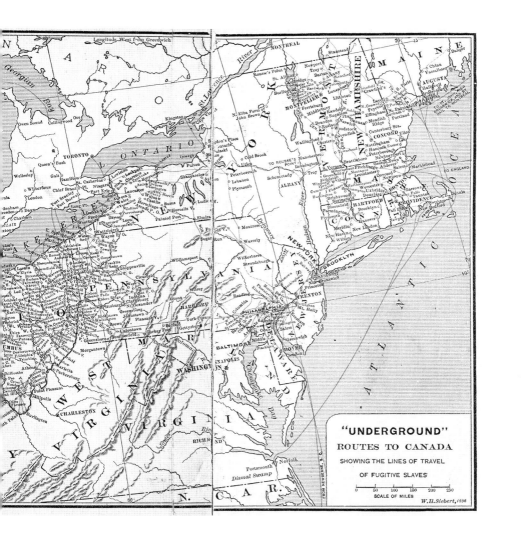

"UNDERGROUND"

ROUTES TO CANADA

SHOWING THE LINES OF TRAVEL

OF FUGITIVE SLAVES

0   50   100   150   200   250
SCALE OF MILES

W.H.Siebert, 1896

Published by The History Press
Charleston, SC
www.historypress.com

Cover images: Painting courtesy of the City of Oberlin, Ohio; the Oberlin High School 2011 Advanced Art Class; and Rosen-Jones Photography. Addison White photograph courtesy of the Booth family of Mechanicsburg, Ohio. Letter from Kentucky slave trader courtesy of National Museum of African American History & Culture, Smithsonian Institution.

Frontispiece: Underground Railroad routes were only in free states and led to Canada. *New York Public Library.*

First published 2023

Manufactured in the United States

ISBN 9781467153201

Library of Congress Control Number: 2022944982

Notice: The information in this book is true and complete to the best of our knowledge. It is offered without guarantee on the part of the author or The History Press. The author and The History Press disclaim all liability in connection with the use of this book.

If there's a book that you want to read,
but it hasn't been written yet,
then you must write it.

—Toni Morrison

CONTENTS

ACKNOWLEDGEMENTS

A long list of people supported me in this endeavor, and I am grateful to all. At the top of the list are the siblings Shari and John Booth, descendants of Addison White; based on very little, they trusted an unknown wannabe author and graciously shared their memories and advice. Their belief in me was as important as the family stories they told and helped spur me on. My son Ben Schulz, an author and former historical reenactor, always helps me in many ways, especially with his extensive knowledge of the nineteenth century. My husband, Ed Schulz, is a supportive partner who believes that everyone should follow their dreams, as well as being a highly competent chauffeur to Underground Railroad sites. We even made a cross-country trip together to reconnect with some of the locations mentioned with no golf involved. In college, Ed was more comfortable in economics classes than in history; his viewpoint has made me mindful of the constant underpinnings of capitalism in our history.

In my quest to get this material published, good friend Susan Boe was invaluable. Susan had two careers: one as a talented journalist and another as an excellent lawyer. She gave her time generously with advice from both of her knowledge bases. Retired editor Debbie Ray also helped hone my writing skills, listened to my frustrations and kept me going. Family friend KiKi Levine gave interesting pointers from the perspective of her field. Several other people from my past got over their surprise at hearing from me and vouched for me or gave information and support. And many more family and friends were generally interested, supportive and fonts of good cheer.

Among the experts on the Underground Railroad I consulted, Dewey Scott deserves a big thank-you. Even by phone, Dewey loves to share his deep knowledge of the John Parker House and the town of Ripley. Happy to speak at length, he is, in his own words, "like a tire rolling downhill." Other tour guides who went out of their way to help me were Howard McClain at the Rankin House and Dale Henry at Springfield's Gammon House.

A very loud shout-out goes to the innumerable librarians and staff members of various historical societies who work very hard to conserve material and cheerfully provide it upon request. There are too many to name, but my colleagues in information services are the best—librarians rock! One of them a *long* time ago filed away a brief summary of a local antebellum incident, allowing me to find it decades later in the basement of the Wittenberg library. It was from this yellowed typed paper that I first learned of the Addison White story, which instantly captivated me even in barebones form. Later on, I was lucky to cross paths with Debbi Young, who has carefully organized and updated the Dohron Wilson scrapbooks in the Mechanicsburg Public Library. Image librarians were also a boon; of that group, Jenni Salamon and the staff of Ohio History Connection stand out. OHC dealt with me generously, quickly eased through small difficulties and made photo selection a breeze.

Behind the scenes, time, talent and funding had already been applied to digitizing thousands and thousands of pages of relevant materials. I owe some unknown people a *huge* thank-you for hand scanning each and every Siebert paper; this book could not have been written otherwise. All through this project, I benefited from the assistance of random Ohioans, Buckeyes being a helpful sort. But an Ohioan with a library degree? *That* will be fabulous service. Ohio's high school history teachers also deserve kudos; many have worked to recover the Underground Railroad events of their communities. Two in particular helped me: Paul LaRue and Cathy D. Nelson. Late in my project, a trio of Lorain County residents—Jon Clark, Tanya Rosen-Jones and Garry Gibbs—swung into gear to allow the book's cover to take shape. Their efforts followed the initial creativity of Oberlin High School students Marissa Hart and Neva Linn Rustad, both of whom are in art careers today. You should not judge a book by its cover, but I can attest that all these people are rock solid and worthy of gratitude.

My relationship with my acquisitions editor John Rodrigue came after much research was done and the book was finally coming together. For this new author, John was a reassuring source of calm, good taste and wise advice. John works absurdly early hours two time zones ahead of me. For any question I had, I always knew that I would wake up to an e-mail containing a cogent, well-thought-out answer—a great launch into a productive day. And with his light touch, he made weighty improvements to your reading experience. Many thanks to John.

INTRODUCTION

The Underground Railroad has enriched our history with marvelous stories. We have inherited tales of well-planned routes that extended as far south as Alabama and Georgia and envision these trails dotted with homes of heroic White station operators. We hear that runaway slaves made their way from one safe spot to the next through dark tunnels or under the stars, humming a drinking gourd song that kept them pointed north. In the daytime, it is said, they occasionally spotted quilts hung on clotheslines, with helpful images sewn in that functioned as Underground Railroad code. When not on the move, they cowered silently in one secret room or another. Good stories all, but the problem is that almost none are true.

The Underground Railroad existed *only* in northern free states. There, help was available for freedom seekers from at least 1800, although no one called it the Underground Railroad then—no one knew what a railroad was much before the 1830s.[1] Few White people participated in the effort until that decade; for years, the Underground Railroad was primarily a system of Blacks helping Blacks. It existed to support the travel of fugitives to the guaranteed freedom of Canada, something even the free U.S. states denied them. Enslaved people in the border states of Maryland, Virginia and Kentucky heard tell of the Underground Railroad but understood that travel to it was risky; they were entirely on their own until they crossed into a northern state. This made the Underground Railroad a practical option only for those living within a walkable distance of it, most often just two or three days. There were a few exceptions, such as river and sea ports enabling connection by boat, but generally the Underground Railroad was unknown in the Deep South.

The state most heavily traveled by people fleeing slavery—for reasons of geography, history and attitude—was Ohio. A map of Underground Railroad travel patterns, as best as can be constructed years after the fact, shows a few specific thoroughfares in eastern states but an intricate spider web of routes blanketing Ohio. Hundreds of fleeing people passed through on each of these Ohio lines. Even the well-meaning and organized opponents of slavery in Philadelphia marveled at the volume of fugitive traffic moving through Cincinnati; other Ohio towns barely heard of back east, places like Ripley and Salem, hosted nearly as much. Numbers are hard to pin down, but more enslaved people seem to have escaped through Ohio than through all other states combined.

I lived most of my life in Ohio, first on a major route in eastern Ohio and then on a confluence of routes north of Cincinnati. In both places, the Underground Railroad was all around yet barely talked about. Perhaps as midwesterners, we just didn't talk about ourselves much. But more importantly, whiffs of Jim Crow, maybe more accurately described as a choking fog, had settled in by my childhood in the 1950s. A northern brand of racism kept Whites silent about what should have been a major point of pride. Although Black people were well in evidence, the people in my social circle were White. Among them, I sensed confusion about the matter. The Underground Railroad era was far distant in time, driven by priorities now absent. Should this antebellum legacy be celebrated or ignored?

In recent years, there has thankfully been renewed interest in the Underground Railroad, although I have sometimes been frustrated with the fictional accounts. In trying to recover the nearly lost history of this era, creators are adding all sorts of colorful embellishments. Besides the inaccurate notions about quilts and songs, they insert magical realism. The whole Underground Railroad effort seems mysterious and otherworldly to us now, so why not tell it magically? The creative license in this genre that bothers me most is the choice of setting. Stories are told of the Underground Railroad in southern slave states, which is very misleading to today's readers. Second to that is a focus on the East Coast, with its powerful media market dating back to the nineteenth century. Yes, Philadelphia has a wonderful antislavery heritage preserved by the likes of Underground Railroad operative and writer William Still, a free Black man. Meanwhile, stories based on the Underground Railroad's major location—the whole state of Ohio—are not being told.

The true stories, to the extent that they can be recovered, are as fascinating as anything fiction writers can imagine. They include elements that might surprise those who have heard only distorted lore. While there are indeed many White people to celebrate, African Americans are the leading characters and heroes of the stories, whether they were free or fleeing slavery. This group did a lot less slinking around and a lot more hiding in plain sight than we have been led to believe. And to add to the confusion about whether real railroads were involved, well, they were. Plenty of well-dressed fugitives posing as free citizens held tickets on trains—or on canalboats—wending their way northward through Ohio ever closer to Canada.

This book will explain *why* Ohio was so prominent in this noble effort, bracketed in between stories of two of Ohio's heroes. Throughout, you will encounter very few secret rooms, tunnels or coded quilts, but you may not miss these legends or even notice their absence because they are supplanted with better qualities: courage and cunning. The valiant strength of the real people who worked to overcome the wickedness of slavery needs no embellishment.

Chapter 1

ADDISON WHITE, UDNEY HYDE AND THE THREE AMANDAS

Addison White knew all about salt. He knew how to harvest brine from a Kentucky salt lick, digging deep holes where a salty liquid would seep in. He knew the weight of the buckets as he drew the brine out and the labor of cutting wood for fires to heat it. He knew to maintain those fires at a steady temperature under the salt pans. Just below boiling was best for fine table salt, but a lower temperature would work for the coarse salt needed for meatpacking.[2] The pork processors in Cincinnati, on the north side of the big river not far away, ordered tons and tons of the stuff. Addison knew to be patient while the crystals formed, unlike the meatpackers always clamoring for more. And Addison White knew another thing about salt that the customers didn't: he knew what it felt like on the ripped flesh of his back after a whipping. Addison White was enslaved.[3]

Salt-making interested Addison. He liked watching the mounds of crystals form, a latent little surprise each time. He had both the mind and body for the work, as he was inquisitive and strong. But no matter—he got whipped some days regardless. There seemed to be no rhyme or reason for the whippings, possibly why it played on his mind so badly. His owner, Daniel Garrard White, had grown up in a family who believed in whipping their slaves. Daniel's father, Hugh Lowery White, was feared by the slaves around Clay County, where the White family had settled after the Revolution to become prominent salt merchants. One later recounted, "Hugh White wuz so mean to his slaves I know of two gals that kilt themselves. One nigger gal Sudie wuz found across the bed with a pen knife in her hand. He whipped another nigger gal most to death for fergitting to put onions in the stew. The next day she went down to the river…and her body finally washed upon the shore."[4] While many slaves of the upper South were spared the very worst beatings of slavery, those owned by the Whites were not.

Even so, Addison had not thought much about running away. The saltworks Daniel White was attempting to develop were in Fleming County; it has never been determined if Addison was born nearby or had been brought out of Clay farther down in the heart of the state. Either way, he was well aware that he could easily walk to the Ohio River in one night, and he had heard about something called the Underground Railroad on the other side. But Addison had a wife and young children. He knew what life was like where he was, and he was not so sure what Ohio—or Canada—offered. Could he support himself there? Those Cincinnati pork-packers ordered their salt from Kentucky—were there no saltworks up north?

One summer day in 1856, the decision to run was made for him. Due to yet another inscrutable infraction, he was to be whipped again. This time, word was that a "nigger breaker" was being brought in to deal with him. Rather than be whipped in an impromptu manner at the saltworks as before, Addison would be taken to a public whipping post. Tied there, he would probably pass out during the slashing strokes. Then more salt. The prospect caused Addison to snap and attack his overseer. About thirty-five years old and much bigger than most men, he easily pushed the overseer to the ground. Addison immediately realized that if he did *not* run, he was as good as dead.

Exactly how Addison managed to escape is lost within that ugly era, but he did get away. Instead of heading directly north to Maysville and the river, he seems to have taken a circuitous route. Perhaps this was cunning; perhaps it was to see and seek aid from loved ones before he went north. He passed through the town of Cynthiana to the west, where he encountered a pretty young Black girl named Amanda Barrow sitting on a porch snapping beans—a common activity in late summer Kentucky. From there he followed a road ending at river's edge across from Ripley, Ohio. With some scavenged wood, Addison floated partway out before swimming the final distance. He knew to look for a set of steep stairs cut into the hill just west of town, which he could just make out in the moonlight. At the top was a small house with a lantern burning in a window—this was Reverend Rankin's house, where they said you could get help.

Common practice in the Rankin home was for Jean Rankin to feed escaping slaves whatever she had and to make sure they were appropriately clothed and well shod. After sizing up new arrivals, she would dig into her boxes of goods, the result of her husband's constant speeches and fundraising, to find what she thought they needed. This was done hastily because you did not tarry long at the Rankins'—everyone on both sides of the river knew that it was an obvious place to look for fugitives. Even before her ministrations had concluded, one of the Rankins' teenage sons would be saddling up and preparing for a night ride into the wooded hills to the north. He took the road and asked his "passengers" to walk off to the side within earshot—the journey was safer that way. Before dawn, the small procession arrived at a station where the fugitives could rest and eat before the process was repeated with a new conductor. By then, the sleepy Rankin boy had returned home. It kept getting a bit easier and safer as the freedom seekers got farther from the river, away from the gaggle of slave catchers and rascals it harbored.

Lore among Addison White's descendants suggests that he reached central Ohio's Champaign County just three days after leaving the Rankins. If true, that one-hundred-mile achievement is surprising but not impossible. An Underground Railroad journey usually took longer; indeed, in safe regions there was no pressing reason for hurry. It is also said that he navigated part of it completely alone, without the aid of anyone else, a circumstance not unheard of. The main takeaway from these accounts—this part undoubtedly true—is that Addison arrived in Champaign County without having developed a clear sense of Ohio, its laws or his own status. Some Black people were free here. Was he free too? The strangeness of the land further unsettled him. The county's name, borrowed from the French, meant open, flat country. Having spent his whole life in Kentucky, Addison had never seen such land. He could now see a patchwork of pastures, cornfields and woodlands stretching on for miles—odd but pleasant, except that it made him feel exposed to everyone else who could see across these gently sloped plains.

Addison's confusion about his freedom, or lack of it, may seem naïve but was not unwarranted. The nation's 1850 Fugitive Slave Law stated that his enslaved status was to be maintained everywhere in the United States; however, thought in Ohio differed. On his journey, Addison had already heard contradictory information. For undeniable, irreversible freedom in 1856, he was supposed to continue on to Canada. But he was also told that Ohioans, like the majority of northerners, hated some slave law that had gone into effect back in 1850. In fact, so many hated it so much that they were happy to disregard and disobey it; they would *not* send him back to Kentucky, as the law specifically *required* them to do. Abhorrence of the awful 1850 law, particularly the part that turned them all into slave catchers,

Top: Addison White. *Ohio History Connection.*

Bottom: Udney Hyde. *Ohio History Connection.*

may explain his fast trip up from Ripley. So many Ohioans were opposed to slavery by 1856 that the Underground Railroad was not really so underground anymore. Transporting fugitives now happened openly and in broad daylight in much of Ohio.

It was in this milieu that Addison White found his way to the home of Udney Hyde in the Champaign County village of Mechanicsburg. Udney Hyde was one of the more colorful characters of the Underground Railroad. Simply stated, he was a badass. While Addison had probably heard a prayer from the devout Reverend Rankin, a Presbyterian, and had been addressed in the "thees" and "thous" of Quakerdom as he passed through the town of Wilmington, Udney Hyde did not give two hoots about anything related to the church. He swore like a sailor, and his only noticeable devotion was his hatred of slavery.

If asked why he detested slavery so much, Udney might share his observation that little black lambs cried every bit as much as white lambs when separated from their mothers, proving to him that color did not matter among the world's creatures. That was if he was in an expansive mood. On another day, he might just tell you to go to hell.

Both of Udney Hyde's grandfathers were prominent officers of the American Revolution. More germane to our story, both were well-born men of New England. Udney's Grandfather Hyde[5] was associated with the village of Hyde Park in northern Vermont; his Grandfather Hay,[6] a personal friend of George Washington's, was involved in Vermont politics. Udney had come to Ohio in the mid-1830s with his new wife, the former Olive Hunter of Connecticut. Their relocation was part of a wave of New Englanders settling eastern Champaign County.

Most of the men in this group were skilled in construction and the trades. Udney was a blacksmith; many others called themselves mechanics. Upon arriving in Ohio, they surveyed their chosen spot—a fertile, verdant expanse drained by a gurgling stream—and decided to name it Mechanicsburg. They were, after all, engineers, not poets. The town became an industrious hive of tool and wagon-making. If you had a wobbly loom, a broken plow or a bent reaper part, Mechanicsburg was a good place to go.

Along with their well-honed tools, the Mechanicsburg mechanics brought with them well-honed Yankee attitudes, meaning they were strongly antislavery. This stance was prominent in the vicinity, but as in much of Ohio, there were competing views. Other nearby settlers from Virginia had brought an acceptance of slavery; these different pockets of settlers did not like each other much. An 1881 county history includes anecdotes about Virginians and New Englanders refusing to do business with each other. Their animus was even evidenced by the sophomoric practice of occasionally throwing eggs at each other. Nearly everyone raised chickens, providing an excess of eggs for those individuals seeking an overt expression of hostility. When eggs weren't enough, fistfights were known to break out outside Mechanicsburg's popular alehouse.

None of this bothered Udney Hyde much because he was as tough as they came. He had started assisting fugitives in 1851, just after the Fugitive Slave Law went into effect; it was just like Udney Hyde to step in at the very moment the federal government firmly dictated that he should not. He had once masterminded the transport of a whole group of twenty-four men, women and children—an accomplishment he was proud of. By the time Addison White walked through his door, Hyde calculated that this was the 513th fugitive he would assist. It was unusual for someone to keep careful track like that, but Hyde hated slavery so much that he had been keeping score, as if he single-handedly wanted to defeat it. He had also become more open in the work. Once when Udney was ferrying Underground Railroad "freight," a southern sympathizer called out, "Whatcha haulin there?" "Got niggers, goddammit!!" was the barked reply as his wagon rolled on unimpeded. It is not clear if Udney was making a ridiculous, off-putting joke, or if he had the attitude of "Well, what of it!?" Probably the latter; in any case, most people left Udney Hyde alone.

But not everyone. Living in the village, Udney had to deal with a few strangers and bothersome, nosey types. For their safety, the Black people staying with him usually slept in a small, difficult-to-reach cellar. Fugitive traffic through Mechanicsburg was high, and the Hydes sometimes hosted sizable groups. Depending on the weather and how many people were present, freedom seekers might sleep in his livery stable or that of his neighbor. One night, the number of his guests had unexpectedly grown by one when a teenage girl on her way to Canada gave birth in his cellar. The next day, excited neighbor ladies appeared with an assortment of old blankets, baby clothes and baked goods. They came offering help, but really, they wanted to see the new Black baby, a novelty no one in Mechanicsburg had ever seen. The African American child born in Udney's cellar is assumed to be the first such birth in the town.

The women were trustworthy, but in case some people passing by were not, Udney had taken the precaution of building a platform partway down his well to serve as an emergency hiding place. His guests ventured outside at times, and this scary perch could be used by one or two of them in a pinch.

One of the town's clever innovators, Udney made his living in several ways. Besides his smithy work, he owned a farm outside of town where he was engaged in turning the oaks, locusts and sweetgums on his back acreage into rails and railroad ties. That was in addition to a bit of corn he grew out front. Previously, he had spent a stint as a clock peddler, selling this quality Mechanicsburg product to the residents of central Ohio. The knowledge he gained of roads and towns may have informed his later antislavery travels.

Of all the Hyde children, it was Amanda who was cut from the same sturdy cloth as her father. She loved to be a part of an Underground Railroad transport, riding on the wagon seat beside her dad. Behind them, the wagon had a false bottom, creating a narrow space where people could lie under its ostensible cargo, offering concealment but little comfort. When it made sense, a more private closed top was added to the back of the wagon. Either way, Amanda was up front with a breeze in her hair and adventure in her mind. She was now a teen, but even when younger, she had been allowed to go on these trips if she didn't have school, although it had made her mother nervous because the route went through Marysville, a town of Virginia sentiment. Her dad sometimes got shot at in that town, and once, she had also. It was a detail the two may have neglected to share back at home.

The intrepid pair and their passengers were usually on their way to the Underground station of John Cratty in Delaware County. Sometimes they went even farther to the Quaker and free Black settlements along Alum Creek, requiring an overnight stay. These deliveries, fifty- and seventy-mile round trips, respectively, were more ambitious than what most Underground

Railroad conductors undertook, but Udney—not to mention Amanda—liked to be out on the road.

Approaching the age of fifty, Udney had grown tired of living in town, where he had to avoid busybodies and a few southern sympathizers. His wife may have preferred living there, but she died in 1854. Udney was considering moving out to his farm, close to his grown son Russell. There he could continue blacksmithing while developing his wood rail business. A bonus would be that any freedom seeker who turned up could move about more openly on the farm during their stays. Udney planned to build a more commodious farmhouse some year, but in the meantime, they could all make do with the simple log house already there.

Addison is believed to have arrived at the Hyde home in town in late August 1856. Udney assured him of safety and a badly needed place to rest but announced that they would be heading north in just a few days. However, that day of transport somehow never came. Addison may have sensed that this family kindly offering assistance was in serious need of help themselves. Everyone in the Hyde home was in grief, particularly the adolescent children still mourning their mother.

The clearest sign of need, however, was Udney Hyde's leg injury, which has variously been described as a broken leg, a broken ankle or a crushed heel. The debilitating injury may have occurred before Addison arrived, although most story versions place it later; it was caused when a log unexpectedly fell on Udney's lower leg. In those days before advanced orthopedic care, it took him a long time to heal. Regardless of the timing, at some point during Addison's stay, the agreement between the two men changed. Now, if Udney suggested Addison should move on to the north for his own good, Addison replied something like, "Well, who's goin to pick yur corn? Who's goin to mind them horses? The youngins caint handle everything." Addison White simply refused to leave. He was fifteen years younger than Hyde, strong and fit, and the family needed help. Udney began paying White for his work, and he stayed through the winter.

While there, Addison bonded with the Hyde family. He missed his wife and children in Kentucky. The Hyde kids were missing their mother. Addison felt particularly bad for eldest daughter Amanda, now saddled with an expanded load of housework. Where he came from, White women often relied on help, but Ohio womenfolk seemed to do a lot of their own chores. He started pitching in as best he could, regularly fetching water and firewood and lending a hand with the rigors of washday. "Mandy and Add" seemed to get on. Truth was, Addison was a kinder, more patient man than her father. There was a gentleness about Addison that the whippings could not touch and had never destroyed. He brought back into the house some of the qualities of her deceased mother.

Before long, one of the Hydes brought up the subject of reading. Addison could not read; would he like to learn? Mandy and Add began huddling over the table with her old McGuffey reader and a slate. She enjoyed teaching him, and he picked it up pretty well, although the fancy scripts of handwriting continued to mystify him (in a later census, he was reported to be a man who could read but could not write). At some point during this education project, Addison got the idea of writing to his wife. His life in Ohio was feeling stable and safe—perhaps she could be persuaded to join him. A letter was drafted by Hyde family friend Charles Taylor. Mr. Taylor thought to question the wisdom of mailing it from the Mechanicsburg Post Office—that would be too obvious if Addison's owner got wind of it. He offered to take the letter— and subsequent ones—to the bigger town of Springfield and mail it from there. Addison's wife, who was also named Mandy, was invited to reply by way of the Springfield Post Office, and Taylor would handle the rest.

A string of letters went back and forth between Kentucky and Ohio that winter. Multiple ones were needed because it turned out that Mandy White had little interest in moving to Ohio. Her thoughts have never been fully explained. Perhaps she was not as fond of Addison as he was of her. She was reportedly a free woman and, in theory, could do what she liked. She had heard of bad things happening in Ohio. In nearby Cincinnati, there had been race riots and beatings of Black people, even *free* Black people. That scared her. Also, was Addison's situation in Mechanicsburg truly secure? What if she took the children to Ohio, only to have him whisked back to his owner? Mandy White was justified in her trepidations. If she had managed the feat of carving out a quiet life in Kentucky where she was left alone, she may have been wise to stay there.

In the end, Addison had to accept that her answer was no—she would not move. But an even bigger disappointment resulted from the letter writing campaign. Using the Springfield Post Office had been a sensible tactic, except that no one realized that its postmaster, William Boggs, was a man friendly to the South. Or maybe he was just a stickler for the law, including that Fugitive Slave Law. In either case, something about the multiple White letters passing through his post office seemed fishy, so Boggs opened one and read it. So much for being lawful.

It was not hard to piece together the basic facts, which Boggs promptly relayed to the U.S. marshal of Cincinnati. There followed two incidents of strangers showing up in Champaign County with suspect stories that, in hindsight, never quite added up. The Hydes had by this time moved to the farm; both the town and the farm were cased. Even so, White stayed with Hyde, refusing to leave. Maybe he felt that the farm was safe. It is not clear how much danger either man suspected, although Udney did give Addison a pistol, something he had never before been permitted to possess. Addison took it to a field and repeatedly practiced with it, perfecting his shot.

Spring was coming on; there was plowing and planting to be done. Hyde was still laid up. By now, many people in the community realized that Hyde had the assistance of some able-bodied man. If they had not seen White directly, it was clear that the farm was being well tended—most likely by a runaway slave, knowing Hyde. And that was fine with them.

Any illusion of Addison White's safety was shattered one chilly morning in mid-May. Shortly after dawn, when only White was up in the Hyde cabin stoking the fire, he heard a noise and looked out the window. There were eight men approaching, three of whom were wearing the uniforms of the U.S. Marshal Service. White quickly darted back up into the small loft where he slept. The log home was not spacious, but this second-story cubicle had been designated for him. The only way one could gain entrance was through a narrow opening approached by a ladder. There was no window. It was a portion of the home that could be guarded like a fortress, especially when one had a gun, as White did.

After their knocks failed to provoke a response, the lawmen burst through the front door, surprising and waking the rest of the house. One of the marshals noticed movement of the loft boards above and fired his shotgun in that direction, creating a hole but missing White. The marshals loudly demanded that White come down. They directed homeowner Udney Hyde to likewise demand it, although he of course refused. Instead, he tried to send his adolescent son Rheuna to the farm next door to get help from elder son Russell. The marshals were suspicious of the ploy and caught the boy, holding him fast.

Addison White, after eight months in Ohio, was now fully aware of the provisions of the Fugitive Slave Law; he realized that Hyde was risking massive legal trouble by protecting him. White had quietly decided that he would rather die than return to slavery, but even that would not absolve Hyde. During the standoff, with marshals below shouting demands and White above aiming his pistol at the opening, White suggested that the visitors put down their firearms and move the dispute to an outside field. Strong and able, Addison White was willing to take them all on unarmed, in a different venue without Hyde in the scene. But no one, certainly not irascible Udney Hyde, much cared for that suggestion.

More negotiation time elapsed. White was clearly not coming down on his own, so one of the marshals determined to go up and get him. He started up the ladder, shotgun in hand, not realizing that White was also armed. As soon as the marshal's head appeared in the opening, White fired his pistol. Fortunately for all involved, the ball glanced off the shotgun barrel before tearing off some of the man's ear tissue in Van Gogh–like fashion. The dazed marshal fell backward to the floor, convinced that he had been mortally wounded.

His equally stunned companions fled outside, offering him no aid. They were unsure what to do and were particularly befuddled by Udney Hyde, who had stayed in bed during the entire altercation. Even after the shooting, he was still in bed. Under his blankets, there was nothing visible about any injury, so through the doorway they asked Rheuna's twin, Amanda, why her father was bed-bound. Decades later, she claimed to have no idea what inspired her response: "He has smallpox." The words burst out of her mouth, seemingly on their own.

Already terrified of the armed Black man overhead, they now had smallpox to contend with as well. It was about this time that Hyde called to Amanda, "Mandy, it's time to go feed the chickens!" Amanda, as quick-witted as her father, knew that he did not give a damn about feeding chickens at that particular moment, but she played along. Grabbing the pail of cracked corn, she plodded out into a damp morning toward the coop. Reaching the chickens, she kept going—on a trot. A marshal noticed and hollered at her, threatening to shoot. The unfazed fifteen-year-old simply ran faster, while one of the men pursued. Fleet of foot, she beat the older man to her brother's house. Thinking that he had no quarrel with whoever this neighbor was and that she was just a scared kid, the marshal left the siblings alone. Russell immediately grasped what was going on and ran to the home of another neighbor who owned a fast horse. With no further communication, Russell hopped on and galloped to town.

Next comes the scene that deserves to be more famous than it is. Like a latter-day Paul Revere, Russell rode through town on the borrowed horse shouting, "Addison White is being taken! Addison White is being taken!" A lot of people who ordinarily pretended not to know Addison White suddenly knew precisely who he was—he had lived among them all winter. He was helping Udney out while Udney was laid up—what good people did. The men and boys of the town—and a few women too—grabbed whatever they could find and headed out through the drizzling rain to the Hyde farm. Pitchforks, sickles, scythes, hay rakes, hoes, carpet beaters, whatever. The mechanics clutched metal rods or their sharpest tools. A large rabble of people brandishing improvised weapons soon appeared at Hyde's cabin.

The wounded marshal had finally collected himself enough to find he had only a bleeding ear and, discerning that he was not about to die, had rejoined his companions outside. Once again a full group of eight, they were confronted by a spokesman for the damp and shivering gang of townspeople, many of whom had not bothered to wear coats. He told the lawmen in no uncertain terms that they had five minutes, and five minutes only, to leave. Seeing no other options, the lawmen did.

The antislavery leanings of Mechanicsburg were well on display that day, and the town had won round one. But the battle was far from over, and everyone knew it. Both Addison White and Udney Hyde left for hiding. It was claimed that Addison had gone on to Canada, but later events suggest that he was really at Cratty's or Alum Creek. Hyde moved here and there over the coming months; he spent weeks in a local swamp, from which he limped to a neighbor's house each night for supper. Once, in order to visit his children, he disguised himself as a madman smeared with mud and twigs. He also left the state for Indiana for a time. Most people were never certain where either man was. Before anyone found out, continued excitement would grip the town.

As expected, two of the marshals returned the following week, accompanied by an even larger retinue. To better manage his father's work, Russell had moved into the log house, where he was arrested with no resistance. Unlike the marshals, Russell seems to have realized that this was a case of mistaken identity. Having bought the smallpox story during their previous visit, the marshals had evidently not gotten a good look at Udney as he remained in bed. They assumed it was Udney Hyde that they were arresting now. The marshals were furious not just with the Hydes but with everyone else around, so the arrests continued. A few locals had noticed the lawmen passing through Mechanicsburg and followed them out to the Hyde farm. One was Charles Taylor, whose letter writing activities had been discovered; he was arrested along with his brother and a friend. The marshals possessed a search warrant for the Hyde home, but they lacked warrants for any additional arrests, which would prove to be problematic for them later. With no apparent concern for the niceties of warrants, the marshals put the four men in a closed carriage and prepared to depart.

Once again, Amanda Hyde sought help. Clutching Russell's revolver, she rode to town on a pony and notified Russell's father-in-law; the news spread swiftly from there. A new group of townspeople confronted the lawmen, distrustful of what was taking place. This time, a local attorney joined the fray. Why were these four people, with little connection to Addison White, being arrested? The questioners were assured that the Fugitive Slave Law justified the arrests, but in any case, the men were being taken to the nearby Urbana courthouse, where charges would be sorted out. Not convinced, some of the townsmen decided to furtively follow. Sure enough, in a few miles, the marshals' carriage veered south off the Urbana road. To the south—if you went far enough—was Cincinnati, a strong proslavery town and the marshals' home base. Much closer than that was the town of South Charleston, on the direct train line to Cincinnati, and this was where the lawmen were heading. Locals did not want to see their compatriots tried in Cincinnati courts or, worse yet, taken to the slave state of Kentucky beyond, where they might simply be killed. One clear-thinking participant headed to the Urbana courthouse to seek a writ of *habeas corpus* mandating their release, along with a warrant for the arrest of the marshals based on their bullying interference. Others began the chase to South Charleston.

Meanwhile, a group in Urbana awaiting the arrival of their arrested friends realized that they had been duped. Men sprinted to the telegraph office, and soon people in various counties were tapping out messages, frantically trying to locate the missing carriage. At least two different posses formed, approaching from opposite locations. Dozens of incensed residents of Champaign and Clark Counties left their homes and farms to search for the dastardly marshals, who represented the Fugitive Slave Law they all hated. Unaware of the humming telegraph lines and the rage that was building, the marshals calmly stopped for a meal at a local tavern with their shackled captives locked out back in an outhouse. In addition to dining, they ran up an exceedingly high liquor bill, an impressive receipt for which was entered into evidence at a later trial. These lawmen were hardly the finest representatives of their profession.

The marshals had avoided traveling obvious routes but were finally apprehended near the National Road, which they had to cross in order to reach South Charleston. Clark County sheriff John Layton had jurisdiction here and informed the marshals of the writ of *habeas corpus*. Full of liquor, they laughingly told him what he could do with his meaningless writ. Undeterred, he reached into his pocket to extract it, causing the marshals to think that he was drawing a gun. Shots were fired, but fortunately a gun jammed. However, the worst injuries occurred when Layton was beaten repeatedly with a billy club; this included several hard blows to the head from which he never fully recovered. At about this same time, a second posse arrived, providing reinforcement.

Eventually, the groups wore themselves out fighting and arresting each other, producing writs and warrants that failed to impress the other side and yielded no resolution. The marshals were able to get away with their detainees, although they realized they were not going to catch any train to Cincinnati that day. The people of South Charleston had been alerted and were coming after them as well. This latter group was new and had fresh horses, an important point in those days. The only thing for the marshals to do was to keep heading southwest in their carriage, hoping to reach Cincinnati one way or another.

It was now dark, and a high-speed chase—nineteenth century style—ensued by lantern light. The groups drove all night, but in the end the horses of the South Charleston boys were too good; also, they had been joined in the wee hours by several butchers from the nearby town of Xenia, careening toward the trouble in meat wagons. Close to dawn, the marshals were overtaken again. They were nearly halfway to Cincinnati, with a different train line out of Dayton just ahead. Save for the fresh horses and the determination of people of multiple counties, the marshals might have gotten away.

Subsequent to the week's events, a dizzying array of arrests, lawsuits, countersuits, motions, countermotions, dismissals and what-have-you were recorded. Hearings and trials were held in the packed courthouses of multiple counties through the summer and into the fall. A portion of these proceedings were transferred, as feared, to the Federal Court in Cincinnati. Some individuals were cleared in one location but then abruptly arrested in another. The beating of Sheriff Layton and the warrantless arrests made by the marshals were important charges, but so, too, were actions taken by locals resisting the marshals in violation of the Fugitive Slave Law. As many as seventy citizens were said to be under investigation.

Raucous public meetings also took place, with dissent expressed and resolutions passed, all breathlessly covered by the press. Local farm boy Bennie Prince was among many who eagerly read accounts of the discord in the local newspaper his father picked up in Urbana each week when he took the eggs to market. Uncommonly bright, young Bennie was amazed that incidents that had taken place on the quiet roads amid villages he knew well now had national import. People said the details had been telegraphed all around and that Addison, Udney and the rest of the drama had been depicted in newspapers as far away as New York City.

If anyone was prescient in all this turmoil, it was the story's more uneducated people. Doubts and confusion about the laws expressed by Addison White and his wife in Kentucky were borne out. What did these laws guarantee? Neither of these African Americans could read the law, but it was soon apparent that educated White men with their shelves and shelves of fat law books could not make much sense of it either. Sorting out everyone's rights in these slavery-related disputes amounted to a huge legal morass.

Due to the involvement of the Federal Court and the U.S. marshals, the main question hinged on who had precedence: the United States or the State of Ohio. This was less settled than we might assume from our twenty-first-century perch. The Dred Scott decision had come down a few months prior, but its convoluted logic wasn't much help. In the aftermath of Addison's and Udney's rescue, a northern state was arguing for states' rights, while the slaveholding world was rooting for federal law. Some in the South rightfully saw this circumstance as a slippery slope; an editorial writer from the *Charleston (SC) Mercury* was one who had pointed out the irony.[7] We can be sure that, like Bennie Prince, a certain lawyer residing in Illinois was also following news reports out of Ohio that summer of 1857. Still unknown to many Ohioans at the time, it would take Lincoln's election to the presidency and a horrific war to resolve the significant questions posed.

But first, matters had to be settled within Ohio. The feds and local law enforcement had applied a lot of legal prowess to the task of arresting each other, and representatives of both sides were in prison. No one was satisfied. The Ohio governor at the time was Salmon P. Chase, a product of Cincinnati's tight-knit antislavery community and a gifted civil rights attorney. Governor Chase, later to serve in Lincoln's cabinet and on the Supreme Court, negotiated a deal that released everyone—perhaps that was the easy way out. This left only one person with a precarious status, that being Addison White. He had not gone to Canada after all, as may have been revealed at one of the trials. Daniel White still claimed ownership and wanted him back. But giving an opening, Daniel White agreed to be reimbursed for his "property." Some northerners vehemently opposed financial transactions of this type, not wishing to participate in the slave trade. The people of Mechanicsburg, however, were exhausted and fed up by the turmoil. They promptly raised $950—the equivalent of about $30,000 today—to purchase Addison's freedom; he received his manumission, or freedom papers, in November. Both Addison and Udney emerged from hiding and returned to Mechanicsburg.

The story might quietly and calmly end there, except that it doesn't. These lively personalities continued to lead interesting lives, refusing to yield the page. When Udney Hyde returned to Mechanicsburg, he learned that a baby boy had been born to a cousin of his in Vermont. The child was named Addison, a name not appearing elsewhere in the Hyde family tree. Udney's story, reported in New England newspapers, had clearly been cheered by his Yankee relatives. But with his fill of both kudos and legal trouble, not to mention lost income, Udney figured that he had done his part for the Underground Railroad and retired from the effort. In 1859, he married a pretty woman thirty years his junior. When the war came along, Udney was keen to sign up and fight for the cause. His leg must have been better, but by 1861, he was over fifty and deemed insufficiently hardy for the army. His wife might have disagreed, as they had six children into Udney's seventies. At least two of his sons, including the ever-helpful Russell, did serve in the Union army.

Just days before cannons fired on Fort Sumter in the spring of 1861, Amanda Hyde also married. Her new husband, Thomas Shepherd, was a scion of a prominent local family of the antislavery persuasion. She capably minded both the home fires and a newborn while he was off fighting in Georgia under General Sherman. Upon his return, their baby production resumed, and his career and civic activities progressed. In 1877, he was appointed postmaster of Mechanicsburg—an honest one, we presume.

Like Udney and Amanda, Addison also found love and married—twice. But while still single, Addison White found something else: fame. With his story so prominently reported, he caught the eye of Frederick Douglass, who invited White to come visit him in Rochester, New York.[8] There, Addison briefly moved in lofty political circles and appears to have made a speech or two on the antislavery circuit. He wore a fine new suit, in which he had posed for a handsome photograph. He was a long way from the Kentucky saltworks and Daniel White!

After the trip, White stayed in touch with Douglass and was strongly influenced by him. President Lincoln and the Union army were starting to allow Black soldiers, and Douglass was helping to recruit. Brave Black men should sign up! Addison was thrilled. He could join up and fight like the White men of the town. The best option, during that summer of 1863, was to go to Massachusetts and join the 54th Infantry unit. Except for its officers, the unit was to consist entirely of Black men. Soon Addison was on his way.

Able Black men from all over the North were heading to Massachusetts. So many turned up that the quota of one thousand soldiers was rapidly exceeded, and the 55th Regiment was added. Nearly all the men who joined these units were literate, and many seemed really, really smart to Addison—he rode up on the train with a lot of recruits in fancy suits who alternated between reading books and chatting about some place called Oberlin College. Possibly accompanying White was his friend Charles Gammon, son of a respected, free Black family who ran an Underground Railroad station in their tidy brick house in Springfield. In total, about a quarter of the men who joined these Massachusetts units had an Ohio connection.

Their eventual posting was near Charleston, in the South Carolina Lowcountry. A portion of White's compatriots fought in the Battle of Combahee Ferry under the unusual command of Harriet Tubman, but it is not known if he took part. We can assume that he was present for the 1863 Battle of Fort Wagner, the group's signature operation made famous by the movie *Glory*. About half of the 54th were killed, wounded or captured; this included the deaths of Charles Gammon and their commander, Robert Gould Shaw. Addison White seems to have made it through the storied struggle unharmed; however, he later fell victim to a decidedly unglamorous affliction. Failing to keep his feet and socks dry in the area's swampy environment, he came down with a bad case of trench foot. His feet became so pained that he could barely walk, landing him in sick bay for several months.[9]

After returning from the war in the fall of 1865, Addison married Mary Lett. Described as a "mulatto," she descended from one of Virginia's early free Black families, many of whom had moved to Ohio. The Letts trace their lineage back to the 1600s to a loving union between a White woman and her one-time slave Bannaka—both unique, accomplished people. She was an unmarried landowner and capable farm manager, and he was an African prince from the Wolof kingdom of Senegal. Benjamin Banneker, the gifted mathematician and astronomer, was a grandson of the pair and seems to have been schooled in these subjects mainly by knowledgeable African ancestors.[10] Mary Lett, Banneker's apparent great-niece, grew up in an established and educated family, but we don't know much more about her; she died young, disappearing from records by 1870. Addison was single yet again, now with two young Ohio-born children.

He worked for a time as a rail splitter, perhaps learning a few tricks of that trade from his friend Udney. Then a better idea occurred to him. His travels had taken him many places: Kentucky, Ohio, New York, Massachusetts,

The Battle of Fort Wagner brought fame to the Massachusetts 54th, Addison White's regiment. *New York Public Library.*

the Carolinas and points in between. In the large cities he had visited, he noticed that the streets were well kept. Horses pulling wagons and carriages passed by continually, and yet the streets were clean. Ruts were tended to as well. He proposed to the Mechanicsburg town fathers that they establish a street department like in the cities. The mechanics of Mechanicsburg liked that idea and agreed to pay him for the work; Addison began maintaining streets and smoothing ruts. The latter could be quite a chore in that day of dirt roads, especially after soggy springs and heavy rains. Possibly Udney Hyde fashioned a road-scraping blade for him to drag along. Addison is also remembered for driving the town water wagon and filling horse troughs.

Young Bennie Prince and another surprise character now reenter the narrative. At the time of the White-Hyde escapades, Prince had been sent from his family farm to study at Wittenberg, a fledgling Lutheran seminary in Springfield. Prince earned degrees in theology and history and remained at the school, serving in many posts, a revered presence. He was largely responsible for developing the small institution into a full-blown college, replacing Latin and Greek with coursework in modern subjects like chemistry and political science. As the college grew, Dr. Prince hosted many dinners for scholars and donors. The cook at these dinners was Amanda Barrow, whom we last saw snapping Kentucky pole beans on a Cynthiana porch. She had come north for the better jobs in Ohio, and she was a good cook. Prince always liked her, as everyone did. They also liked her succulent roasts, her mushrooms in butter, her vegetable casseroles and her cakes and pies and warm fruit cobblers. She spent a lot of time in the Prince home, where the children, who enjoyed teaching as much as their father did, tried to get Amanda to read as well as she could cook. That was a high bar, one perhaps not reached.

It may have been through "Bennie" Prince that Barrow made the acquaintance of Addison White—for the second time. Whether the two had ever met or not, Prince certainly knew about Addison White out in his home county. Another role Prince may have played is helping Amanda achieve her dream of opening a restaurant; sometime in this era, her eatery appeared on the main street of Mechanicsburg, where it was appreciated by residents and visitors alike. Addison likewise became a fixture of the town. Everyone knew Add White, riding by tipping his hat, his two faithful dogs beside him on the wagon seat. The townspeople even knew the dogs' names were Greeley and Major—interesting choices.[11] Horace Greeley was a New York colleague of Frederick Douglass and an important antislavery voice. Major Martin Delaney, who like Douglass recruited for the Massachusetts 54th, was an unusually talented person, the only Black man advanced to his rank in the Civil War. Addison would have admired, and possibly met, both. Was he demonstrating his political views in the names of his pets?

Amanda Barrow's probable birth date was 1844, making her about two decades younger than White. It was said that she had been brought to Ohio by her father, a Union soldier, although the veracity of the story or who that soldier may have been is unclear. However it happened, Amanda found her way to Springfield and then Mechanicsburg, marrying Addison White in 1879. She soon gave birth; it appears she also raised the offspring from his union with Mary Lett.

It is through Amanda that the stories of Addison White were passed down to his many descendants. Among these anecdotes was the story of how they had chatted while she snapped beans, never imagining that they would meet again, and how years later she would rub her homemade salves into the scars of his back, which were often uncomfortably tight. Amanda, who outlived her husband by fifty years, was an exceptionally capable woman. Besides running her restaurant, she catered events and cooked in the town hotel. A successful businesswoman, she was civically active. In that day, history was envisioned as a series of male achievements; nonetheless, Amanda White is listed in the 1917 Champaign County history as the sole founder of its first

African Methodist Episcopal Church.[12] Late in her long life, this former slave enjoyed listening to her new radio and reading newspapers, proving that the Prince children had done their job well enough. This time was spent relaxing in her favorite rocking chair in a comfortable home, one of several properties she owned. Upon her 1935 death, her obituary ran in various papers, including the *Cincinnati Enquirer*.

Benjamin Prince did not have the opportunity to read his friend's obit, as he had died two years prior, having similarly left a mark on the world. We are indebted to Prince, who sat down in 1907 at the fiftieth anniversary of the White-Hyde events and penned an article about it for the *Ohio Archaeological and Historical Quarterly*. Working both from memory and from old printed sources,

Amanda Barrow White, third wife of Addison White, was a successful businesswoman and civic leader in Mechanicsburg. *Ohio History Connection.*

Dr. Benjamin F. Prince, professor of history and political science, wrote what remains one of the best accounts of "The Rescue Case of 1857."

Prince had little to say about Daniel White of Kentucky, who over time was relegated to footnote status. This is not what his family had expected. Daniel Garrard White carried not one but *two* names of that state's salt royalty, his middle name Garrard being the second. The Whites and the Garrards were not related but probably had business dealings around the time of Daniel's birth. The Garrards were an important political family in the state, and Daniel's middle name seems to have constituted a political statement by the Whites. But good feelings between the families did not last. In later years, there was a falling out between the Whites and Garrards, causing them to wage a longstanding feud, as Kentuckians were wont to do.

Neither illustrious name saved Daniel Garrard White. His saltworks in Fleming County appear to have failed; by 1870, he had moved to West Virginia, seeking a foothold in the oil business. There was oil in Pennsylvania, but down those same mountain ridges in West Virginia, White did not find any. He never received much inheritance either. He was the last born in a very large family, and money only went so far. In 1880, White left his family for the mountains of Colorado to work as a miner and pan for gold.[13] At sixty-one, he was too old for this work. A successful man of that age with his connections should have been back in Kentucky enjoying a bourbon and steak. Instead, he was going hungry in Colorado. That was the worst possible outcome for not producing ore or nuggets, although a more appropriate punishment for Daniel White might have been a whipping.

While Daniel White was out west scratching rocks, Addison White—with his horse, his wagon and his dogs—was rambling through the streets of Mechanicsburg, sometimes stopping for a piece of his wife's apple pie. But Addison and Amanda did not have many years together. During the winter of 1884–85, Addison White and Udney Hyde both died within weeks of each other. Throughout his varied career, Udney had primarily considered himself a blacksmith. Throughout Addison's adult life, as he told the Union army when he enlisted, he considered himself a salt-maker—a good salt-maker. Addison White knew all about salt. After he left Kentucky, though, his life changed. In Ohio, Addison never produced a single grain of salt. Instead, he crafted a life story for his descendants to savor—and for the rest of us to admire. Addison White lived a crucible of a life but emerged with a spirit that was crystalline and pure. His heart remained open to the good, unmarked and unbound from the horrors of slavery.

Chapter 2

OHIO AND THE NATION, 1785–1815

O hio was always destined to be the center of the Underground Railroad, ages before Addison White appeared on the scene. First came the glaciers that smoothed out the bulk of the state, leaving rich soil and arable land that would attract Americans from the original colonies many millennia later. Navigable waterways also beckoned west. When the glaciers melted, they created the Great Lakes connected to the St. Lawrence in the north but left intact an important river system to the south. Seneca Indians called this the "Good River," or Ohi-yo. Anglo settlers later agreed with that assessment, happy to leave rugged eastern lands and float down the beautiful river to establish new farms and towns along its banks. As more and more arrived, villages spread up the river's tributaries and into Ohio's core.[14]

These new settlers who disembarked on the starboard side of their voyage were coming to a region that had been designated slave-free as early as 1787—even before the United States had a constitution. The first survey lines in Ohio had been drawn two years before that, as leaders of our country foresaw a western migration of its population and prepared for land sales. The initial surveying began at the nexus of the Ohio River with the Pennsylvania and Virginia state lines. Starting at that point across from today's West Virginia panhandle, land was gradually set off in neat square townships and sections—no small feat over that area's abundant hills. Based on the numbering scheme used, this area of eastern Ohio was termed "the Seven Ranges"; it would play a prominent role in the Underground Railroad.

The lands newcomers viewed on the river's opposite bank were far different in that they allowed slavery, setting the scene for the drama to come. This southerly territory was all part of the original colony of Virginia, although its western reaches had recently been rechristened Kentucky. There were many White folk already living in Kentucky, which had a couple decades' head start on Ohio in attracting White settlers. Its original association with the powerful Virginia colony was one reason; another was the presence of salt—the very licks worked by Addison White and other enslaved people. Salt was essential for food preservation in the days before refrigeration; not only did it attract entrepreneurs, it also allowed civilization to develop in its vicinity. A population without salt could not thrive.[15] A third reason Kentucky settlement predated Ohio's was its relative lack of Indian habitation. When Virginia colonists began spilling out of the Appalachians trekking west, they encountered grassy rolling plains but few natives. Not that the Indians did not value this land; on the contrary, they regarded it so highly that various native groups had agreed not to live there but rather to share it as a seasonal hunting ground, consistent with their concept of communal landownership. The Iroquois called this place of abundant game drawn to the salt licks and grasses Ken-tah-tee. But neither they nor other Indian tribes were full-time residents; White men were able to wrest control of this "Bluegrass area" with minimal bloodshed. The timing of this takeover is apparent from the name of an important early settlement: in June 1775, founders who were thrilled to learn of the successful opening battles of the Revolution at Lexington and Concord named their new town Lexington. The population grew, and Kentucky would reach statehood by 1792.

The men who had fought at Lexington and Concord, and other New Englanders, were much more interested in Ohio lands than in Virginia-associated Kentucky. New Englanders, some of whom had seen the Ohio Valley during the American Revolution, took the lead in promoting and investing in the region north of the Ohio River. Aware of the surveying underway out west, a group of them gathered at the Bunch of Grapes Tavern in Boston in the spring of 1786 to discuss how to best profit from the opening of Ohio. Their response was to form the Ohio Company of Associates and buy their own land, the next huge tract available downriver from the Seven Ranges. Virginians, including George Washington, saw promise in these Ohio regions and invested; however, it was the New Englanders, some of them clergymen, who drove its initial development. They made certain to insert a nonslavery clause in the 1787 Northwest

Ordinance; the very next year, they mounted an expedition to the confluence of the Muskingum and Ohio Rivers to establish a settlement. This became Ohio's first town of European descendants, who named it Marietta for Marie Antoinette. It may seem odd that these practical and hardy New Englanders looked to a fancy French queen for inspiration, but she was rightfully given credit for facilitating French assistance during the American Revolution. And counter to her image, she simplified French court fashion and manners and was not then, or ever, known to comment on the cake-eating habits of peasants. Her reputation would later suffer during her own country's revolution.

The New England foothold in Ohio was further evidenced by the claims of Connecticut. That state insisted that its original colonial borders extended far, far to the west, all the way to the Mississippi River. New York and Pennsylvania sat in that path and would never agree with their neighbor, but when it came to Ohio, compromise was possible. A certain portion of northern Ohio, bordering Lake Erie, was set aside in recognition of Connecticut's claims. The Connecticut Western Reserve was soon surveyed by Moses Cleaveland, who also founded an early town there; years later, a printer disliked fitting that name on his masthead and dropped one letter. The name shrank as the city on the lake grew.

The Northwest Ordinance of 1787 could control slavery, but it could not control the Indians; the region was slave-free long before it was Indian-free. Americans knew that the land in Ohio was good and were eager to move there. But there were Indians! And they were not necessarily friendly. Reports of attacks and even massacres on the Ohio frontier were publicized in eastern newspapers. Revolutionary general Arthur St. Clair, governor of the Northwest Territory, was thought to be the ideal leader to improve its safety. Instead, his faults added to the mayhem. Something like an early General Custer, St. Clair had an overconfident disregard for the Indians and was hapless as a general. On a 1791 mission north of the brand-new town of Cincinnati, St. Clair and his troops were completely routed by the Indians, who had consolidated forces of many tribes and benefited from the leadership of Chief Little Turtle of the Miamis and Blue Jacket and Tecumseh of the Shawnees. The news shocked easterners: clearly Ohio was not yet safe for White men and women. It fell to General "Mad Anthony" Wayne to redress the problem three years later and eliminate hostile natives. With well-trained, superior forces, he was victorious in northwest Ohio in August 1794 in what was called the Battle of Fallen Timbers. The following summer, a treaty was signed, shoving the Indians out of most of Ohio. The small trickle of White settlers prior to 1795 instantly grew to a gush. "Ohio fever" took hold all over the East. Good land was available out west, and a new sense of safety prevailed. People poured in.

Many of the people who came to Ohio were Revolutionary veterans. The fledgling country had never had sufficient funds to pay them properly, but now there was land—something like 4 million acres of it in the Northwest Territory. With plenty to give away, land grants were offered to veterans with substantial service. At this point, Virginia finally asserted itself, claiming that its large population, specifically its many veterans, might get short-changed. All those millions of acres—what if there wasn't enough? What if land ran out before all its eligible veterans had received their allotments? Consequently, another huge tract was set aside in southern Ohio. This Virginia Military District, similar in size to the Connecticut Western Reserve, ran from the Ohio River northward and was easily reached from Virginia and other points south.

Of course, America being America, frenzied financial action accompanied these land designations. There was much buying and selling of acreage coupled with speculation. For one thing, some Revolutionary veterans preferred to sell their claims and not relocate. Similarly, a part of the Western Reserve was carved out for the residents of specific Connecticut towns that the British had burned to the ground during the Revolution. Most of the recipients quickly figured out that it was more lucrative to sell their shares in the "Firelands" (still called that today) rather than move. Meanwhile, the Ohio Company and other similar ventures were surveying and selling to all comers. Surveying and selling. A land office opened up in the thick of the action in Steubenville, making transactions convenient for newcomers. Ohio Fever raged on and business was hot.

Unlike some of the shameful deceptions of our nation's pecuniary past, publicity about Ohio's fertile land was generally based on fact. Much of the Ohio land really was better—whether compared to rocky New England or to the tobacco-tired soils of Virginia. It was definitely easier to cultivate than the wide Appalachian swath that passes through Pennsylvania and other states. So the message continued: Go to Ohio! This period constituted our country's first westward mania.

By the early 1800s, there were enough people in Ohio to take up the matter of statehood, and delegates were selected for a state constitutional convention. Among those voting was Christopher Malbone, who as a paid servant of the powerful Putnam family of Marietta also went by the name

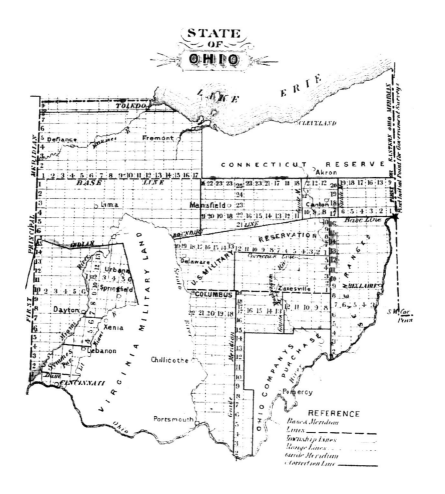

Ohio was carved up for allotment in different sections. *Wikimedia Commons.*

Kitt Putnam. The vote of Kitt Putnam was recorded and counted equal to all other men present. This noteworthy occasion is regarded as the first vote of a free Black man in the Northwest Territory.

Ohio was clearly on its way to becoming a state, but not without some final drama. At the constitutional convention, some of its residents who had originated in Virginia and remained in communication with Thomas Jefferson launched a belated effort to change the state's course. Ohio's new constitution did not have to agree with the old Northwest Ordinance on

The first federal land office in Ohio still stands in Steubenville. *Columbus Public Library.*

the matter of slavery because the new language would supplant it—why have any clause at all about slavery? When that proposal went nowhere, they offered a compromise position of allowing slavery but only up to a certain age. Older African Americans in Ohio would be free. The territory's antislavery contingent rose up and worked diligently to squelch these ideas. One of the most important delegates in this effort was Ephraim Cutler, who had relocated from Massachusetts. He always regretted his lack of education, as the war had interfered with his opportunity to attend Yale. Although embarrassed that he struggled to write well, he was nonetheless widely admired for his common sense, good-natured personality and innate ability. In the heat of the slavery debate, he rose from a sickbed to address the conference and exert his considerable influence. His writing may have been poor, but he seems to have had no difficulties speaking effectively. The vote followed, and in spite of his exhaustion, Cutler insisted on being present. In the end, language copied almost verbatim from the Northwest Ordinance banning all slavery was approved for the new state constitution. The measure passed by one vote.

Ohio thus became a state—a free one—in 1803. Unbeknownst to the delegates debating its constitution, Robert Livingston was simultaneously negotiating with the French for the purchase of the Louisiana Territory. This momentous transaction, and the gain of the major port of New Orleans, created lucrative commercial opportunities for the new upstream state, along with new opportunities for exploitation of the enslaved.

Antislavery views, though not universal, were dominant in Ohio, where several specific categories of residents tended to harbor them. First off were all those Revolutionary veterans. It cannot be claimed that all were opposed to slavery, but many had received an education about Black men during the war. In recent years, America has thankfully been rediscovering the large number of African Americans who fought in its Revolution—and in other early wars as well. Picturing all members of the Continental army as White descendants of Europe is simply incorrect. For example, about 6 percent of men at Valley Forge the winter of 1777–78 were soldiers of color, perhaps a close approximation of the makeup of army as a whole.[16] But that was just the regular army; scores more served their local communities as minutemen. Moreover, the percentage of African Americans in the military grew significantly as the war wore on, with both the Americans and the British aggressively signing up Black men to fill the ranks. By the 1781 Battle of Yorktown, an observer noted that about 25 percent of American troops on the field were Black.[17] A few New England Blacks even served as officers—something that sorely surprised Virginian George Washington, but he adjusted. Those officers would have joined the military as free men, unlike the many enslaved African Americans who served in exchange for the promise of personal freedom. The record of fulfillment of those promises is mixed; many enslaved men did earn their freedom through military service, although some pledges were later revoked.

As a consequence of this service, Whites and Blacks routinely fought together. In nearly all cases, units were racially integrated; only Rhode Island organized segregated units, mostly because they had a very high number of Black soldiers and sailors. Few people gave this integration much thought, and as in all wars, bonds developed. Attitudes varied by region, but White war veterans would have emerged from military service with a familiarity with Blacks they may have lacked previously and a regard for them that ranged somewhere between grudging acceptance and appreciation. These attitudes were later carried to Ohio.

Just like White military veterans who relocated to Ohio, so did some veterans of color. Not all who had served qualified for a land grant, but among those who did, it appears that there were a few Blacks. Bazabeel Norman, possibly Ohio's first Black landowner, served as an artilleryman for four years and was subsequently awarded land near Marietta, along with a gun, a mule and a monthly pension.[18] Another land recipient was Richard

Stanhope, who had functioned as one of George Washington's personal wartime valets. After the war, he had returned to Mount Vernon and was given supervisory duties of the house servants. As a free man, he then moved to Ohio's Virginia Military District. He began preaching as a Baptist minister and changed his name from the previous Stanup to Stanhope. Stanhope lived a very long life and ended up a landowner in the other end of Champaign County from Udney Hyde and Addison White, where he was well known and fondly remembered. A photo taken of him not long before his 1862 death shows snowy white hair and a gentle patrician bearing.[19]

In addition to military veterans of color, many other African Americans without military service came to Ohio in the early 1800s. Most were recently freed slaves who landed in the new state for a variety of reasons. As numbers of slave-owning White Virginians left their homeland for Ohio, they had to make a decision. Of course the slaves could be sold, but some owners preferred to bring them along, freeing them in the process. Their motivation might have been benevolence, but it may also have been expedient to maintain a ready workforce—freedom for Blacks was the result either way. Other former slaves came to Ohio independent of their former owners. A segment of Virginia's population was growing increasingly uncomfortable with slavery; neither Washington nor Jefferson could much defend the ugly institution. Some owners who could afford to do so freed their slaves—either as a group or in selected individual cases. Many of the mass manumissions occurred upon an owner's death, as dictated in a will. In the cases of living Whites freeing individuals, owners tended to be discriminating and usually gave considerable thought to a worker's ability to earn a living. Black men who were trained as blacksmiths, carpenters or in some other trade were the common types manumitted. Slaves working in the trades also had the opportunity to buy their freedom. It was common for such men to work against a quota; production beyond that baseline went toward their personal savings. A few enslaved male musicians and performers who had the flexibility of travel and tips similarly achieved liberty; enslaved preachers had similar mobility.[20] It was more unusual for an enslaved woman to be selected for freedom or to find an avenue to earn it.

No matter how an enslaved person came to be free, it was seldom practical for them to remain in a slave state. The constitutions of southern states were written assuming an enslaved condition for Black people. If he did not leave, a free Black man could find himself engulfed by slavery once again. Virginia and Kentucky laws allowed such a person a few months of safe residency; after that, he could be legally sold. The obvious solution was to leave. Ohio, with good land plentiful and freedom written into its constitution, was the logical place to go.

These forces drew many free Blacks to Ohio. Almost simultaneously, non-free runaways would follow, but that is jumping a bit ahead in our story. At this point, we should just note that the large assemblage of free Blacks was necessary to facilitate the arrival and movement of the latter.

The sizable influx of free Blacks did something else: it began to give White Ohioans pause. Many Ohioans felt that freedom was all to the good, and slavery, as the New England clergy had preached, was all to the bad. But some then said, "Yes, but do we really want all these dark-skinned people around?" Even the New Englanders were slightly alarmed as they realized the Blacks arriving from Kentucky and Virginia were of a social stratum different from the educated, cultured sort they had been used to encountering on the streets of Boston and other northeastern towns. Ohio saw itself as a White state and wanted to stay that way. Black people must be kept at bay. After achieving statehood in 1803, some of Ohio's earliest legislative actions put tight reins on its citizens of color.

From 1804 to 1807, the state passed a series of restrictive laws applying only to "negroes" and "mulattoes." Initially, such people had to produce papers proving that they were free and register all their family members with their county clerk at twelve cents per name. In 1807, this requirement was changed to a $500 bond guaranteeing their good behavior. There were additional serious fines for anyone harboring runaways.[21] Defenders of the state of Ohio point out that these laws were rarely enforced. After all, $500 was a ridiculous sum of money—valued over $10,000 today. A few wealthy people who freed slaves complied with the requirement, but in most cases, it was out of the question and largely ignored. The main point of the financial provisions was to serve as a check on the Black population. If someone's behavior was not good, if he was regarded as "uppity" or a troublemaker, then these laws were available for meting out some punishment—or banishment from the state. People of color got the message that if they wanted to avoid the negative effects of Ohio's "Black Laws," they better blend in quietly and not make waves.

Another Black Law, enforced for forty-two years, was likely the worst of all. It stated that "no negro or mulatto shall testify in a Court of Justice or Record, where the party in cause pending is White." Thus people of color had no recourse if one of their community were attacked, robbed or killed by a White person. This left them sitting ducks for whatever assault an unscrupulous person or crazed mob chose to inflict. Again, in defense of Ohio, a number of White politicians took offense to this law and worked diligently for repeal, particularly Salmon P. Chase of Cincinnati. In 1849, they finally succeeded in removing this statute, although Black people could still not serve on juries or attend White schools. However, the latter restriction was disregarded in some egalitarian-minded communities, such as Mechanicsburg.

It would be tempting to interpret Ohio's strength in the Underground Railroad as proof of its enlightened attitudes and to credit Ohio with helping the nation similarly progress, but the fact is that the state was a disappointment to many of the newly arrived Blacks, for reasons that should be obvious. Most reported that life in Ohio was only marginally better than whatever slave state they had come from. One reported that he had mixed more comfortably with Whites in Alabama; another said that she had felt protected in Kentucky by Whites who knew her but that she never experienced feelings of safety and acceptance in Ohio even after many years.[22]

Quakers constituted another category of newcomer to Ohio that deserves special mention. Many Americans entertain the notions that all Quakers were abolitionists and that all Underground Railroad operatives were Quakers. Neither idea is true. Quakers as a group did tend to be against slavery, but a few of them—admittedly not the norm—actually owned slaves. And they never had a monopoly on Underground Railroad work— other groups were similarly involved. In spite of these caveats, it is indeed true that the antislavery work of Quakers was important; their arrival in the area corresponded to the beginnings of Ohio's Underground Railroad.

Quakers are generally associated with Pennsylvania, but in the early days of this country, they lived many other places as well. Interestingly, there were thriving Quaker communities in the South, in places like Frederick, Maryland; Culpeper, Virginia; and in the Carolinas and Georgia. Over time, these communities dwindled as Friends became disenchanted with their southern environments and moved away. This migration is explained not so much by a change in Quaker thought as by the economic and cultural changes around them. Early in our colonial history, slavery could be found all over the Eastern Seaboard, but by the Revolution, it was dying out in the North while becoming cemented as the economic basis of the South. Not to be underestimated was Eli Whitney's 1794 patent of the cotton gin. His design was brilliantly simple, as many good inventions are, so that the device was widely copied all over cotton lands in just a few years (with little to no profit to Whitney). This completely changed the cotton market and almost overnight turned the United States into a boom producer. As cotton was exported, huge numbers of slaves were imported—a point of controversy both here and in England. The latter country did not allow slavery but was heavily involved regardless through its shipping. In 1807, both countries passed laws prohibiting the international slave trade, shutting off the flow of slave ships to the United States. While well intentioned, these bi-continental laws had a curious effect. The legislation did nothing to reduce America's regional reliance on slave labor. After 1807, the slave population in the United States was regarded by southerners as a valued but limited resource that needed to be aggressively bred and developed. Slave trade *within* the country increased. Cotton was not profitably grown in the upper South, but money could be made by selling slaves from there to the deeper South. Land was wearing out anyway in many Tidewater locations—why not sell some slaves? At one time, many slave owners had resisted breaking up families, but it now became common. Black women were further dehumanized by slave owners who openly judged their ability to conceive and applied the prized descriptor "good breeder" in sale ads. Many American legislators had hoped that the 1807 law presaged the end of slavery, but ironically, it probably became an even more horrible experience.

The Quakers of the upper South sensed these changes early; they also admired the antislavery clauses of the Northwest Ordinance and the new Ohio constitution. Some began to relocate. As the trend picked up, declining membership in the meetinghouses of the South compounded the exodus. Southern Quakers watched their communities lose vibrancy and knew that the action in their faith had gone north. Land between their border state locations and the Ohio Valley was rugged, but once they got to Pittsburgh, it would be an easy glide down the Ohio River. More and more left.

Pennsylvania Quakers also felt the pull west. Unlike their border state neighbors, they did not have to compete in a slave economy, but the better, flatter land of Ohio would be a boon regardless. No one was setting aside special land for them—they were not from Connecticut, and most, as pacifists, were not military veterans. But they went anyway. They had to buy land, so they looked to the closest, most convenient land to reach—on the western side of the river just out of Pennsylvania. This Seven Ranges land was the first in Ohio to be surveyed, and members of the Society of Friends were among the first buyers. It did not hurt that some of the early surveyors and land office employees in eastern Ohio were themselves Quaker. As early as 1801, an organized influx of Quakers had purchased land and established a monthly meeting across the river from Wheeling. Within four years, they could boast of a dozen more nearby meetings, as the three counties stacked up against the Ohio River in eastern Ohio became dominated by Quakers.[23] (Today, this area abuts the West Virginia panhandle, but we need to remind ourselves that land east of the river was Virginia prior to 1863.) The presence of Quakers along the easily navigated Ohio River would have a strong impact on the Underground Railroad.

Quakers were not the only group to migrate from other regions into Ohio. To give the South its due, some southerners were repulsed by the slavery they saw around them. They may have held a minority view in their locales, but together they formed a small but influential influx into Ohio. An example is Presbyterian minister Reverend James Gilliland of South Carolina, who expounded against slavery as early as 1796. That did not go over well in his community; he was expelled from his synod in 1805. Gilliland went north, accompanied by a few of his congregants, and settled in southwest Ohio. Reverend John Rankin of Tennessee, also a Presbyterian, arrived a few years later. Other clergy and laypersons with similar views were dribbling out of the upper South. Thus Ohio's river counties attracted various southern antislavery thinkers. Their aversion to slavery was not abstract; they had personally seen it while growing up, some in their childhood homes. They understood the basic brutality of the peculiar institution, even when they were aware of random spots of kindness and caring that arose between the races caught up in it. They were also realistic about the challenges of eradicating the evil system, which was becoming more and more imbedded in the homelands of their birth. Their early presence in southern Ohio seeded the area with antislavery principles that would take root and flourish as the nineteenth century wore on, turning the area into a veritable Underground Railroad hotbed. The main downside of this relocation was the loss of their ethical voices within the South as its population became more universally aligned with slavery.

The true beginnings of the Underground Railroad are hard to discern. Slaves have always fled; some certainly found their way north into Ohio from Kentucky and Virginia as far back as the eighteenth century. Before 1810, their numbers may not have been high. Those who came in that era were likely seeking freedom within the United States, as the pattern of going to Canada was not yet well established. Nor was there any organized system of assisted travel for freedom seekers, only individual homes and communities here and there where they could hope to find food and rest. Primarily, they found support in areas of African American settlement, although some Quaker areas of eastern Ohio were also in play. With no organization, the only thing linking any of these locations was word of mouth. But conveniently, both populations offered visible clues of identification. Darker skin was an obvious invitation for fugitives to approach—so too were the unique hats and clothing of the Quakers.

After 1810, important changes took place. Of major importance was the War of 1812. It produced yet another group of military veterans—both White and Black—who fought together, a portion of whom settled in Ohio after the war just as their fathers' generation had. But the change prompted by the War of 1812 was more profound than just that. It was mainly fought in northern climes near the Canadian border, much of it a maritime war. Whether on land or sea, a number of Americans from warmer regions experienced the North for the first time through the war. Because White soldiers from slave states were often accompanied by servants, this included Black men. Some enslaved servants had previously been told wild tales about northern abolitionists being monsters who encouraged slaves to escape north so that they could be cooked and eaten. If anyone believed this malarkey, a little time spent along the St. Lawrence disabused them of these strange notions and revealed a society operating smoothly without slavery. Those who got as far north as Canada saw even more of this economic system built solely on paid labor. More importantly, they learned that a country called Canada existed—before the war, many enslaved people had not heard of it. Here was a whole different country with laws granting equal rights to settlers of any color—an epiphany to many. Even some White soldiers and sailors were struck by its difference from their homelands and returned home remarking not just on its cold climate but on how life was lived there. The story of this free land to the north filtered down throughout the slave community and spread hints about another way of life available—for those who could reach it.

Chapter 3

BLACKS, QUAKERS AND INDIANS IN THE EARLIEST YEARS OF THE UNDERGROUND RAILROAD

A s soon as the Ohio River leaves Pennsylvania, it bends sharply to the south, its course firmly dictated by the slanted ridges of the Appalachian Mountains. This general southwest heading continues for well over two hundred miles into the hilly reaches of today's Lawrence County. There the river finally frees itself from the ridge and meanders toward flatter land. As it does so, it angles to the north, creating a soft wedge at Ohio's base. This southernmost point looks like it might be trying to pry Kentucky away from the Virginias, a task it has not been able to accomplish even after centuries. Instead, Lawrence County succeeded at something else. Easily reached from both of the slaveholding states that nearly surround it, the projection attracted an influx of Black settlers early in Ohio's history.

When the first of these settlers of color arrived is unclear, but by 1813, a group had formed the Macedonia Missionary Baptist Church, Ohio's first religious institution specifically for Blacks. The church was in Burlington; the larger town of Ironton nearby hints to the occupation of some of its men. Iron ore was yet another feature of those hills; jobs were available at forges, with iron entrepreneurs happy to pay Black men the reduced wages they were known to settle for. The work was hellish and grueling, but the community offered its protections. The White wealth of Ironton did not take kindly to slave catchers snooping around, potentially interfering with their cheap labor force. In later years, a few of these White town leaders, such as John Campbell,[24] went on to use their significant resources to actively assist the Underground Railroad. Furnace owners relied on and appreciated their

Some of Ohio's earliest Black residents settled in Lawrence County. *HMdb.org.*

Black workforce; over time, the motives of some appear to have evolved beyond economic self-interest all the way to altruism.

The community of Poke Patch once existed about thirty miles to the north of Ironton, situated near Dirty Face Creek and also near Negro Creek. Those names have to tell you something. In addition, the sister community of Blackfork was within a walkable distance. Both communities consisted solely of African Americans.[25] The two settlements shared the aptly named Union Baptist Church, established in 1819. Many of the residents in these places were hiding—either from slave catchers or from Ohio's Black Laws. Back in the day, southern Ohio had a number of Black communities tucked in the hills commonly called "nigger camps" at the time—my guess is that Negro Creek has had its name sanitized as well. In secluded locations, African Americans achieved safety by living among one another, albeit in poor conditions. The Poke Patch group had found its way to an area no one else wanted because it had poor soil and was infested with pokeweed, a poisonous nuisance. Somehow they eked out a life there, although it is now hard to envision because their cabins and fields disappeared long ago. Also gone are most of the additional furnaces that sprang up in the area, offering paid work.

This section of southeast Ohio was one of the first areas of the state where freedom seekers could find safe harbor.[26] Various communities like these extended from Lawrence County up the river toward Pennsylvania and the Mason-Dixon line, forming pockets of Black people helping other Black people. (One of these communities of note is Lett Settlement, the probable birthplace of Addison White's second wife.) A covert Black traveler could mix into a community like Poke Patch inconspicuously. Compared to the named Underground Railroad of later decades, there was zero organization to this early aid—and it was nothing fancy. No wagons with hidden compartments, maybe no wagons at all. No special rooms or hiding places. There was no system, and if there had been a system, no one would have known what to call it. "Railroad" was not a term in use, railroads not yet being a thing. And aid to travelers was rarely "underground" in any sense in the early days. It was just Black people helping Black people by incorporating them into their lives as they passed through.

None of this is meant to diminish the importance of the aid offered. Many, many fugitives found safety, temporary or permanent, in the homes and communities of other Black folk. In order to retrospectively recognize this hospitality and give credit, we now call this the early Underground Railroad, even if no one called it that then. Throughout the whole history of the Underground Railroad, this was the primary way fugitives *did* get help—from other Black people. These other Black people were often encountered in a somewhat random way because specific routes were not well established. To get from Burlington to Poke Patch, the only directions travelers got were to go north for thirty miles until they entered a valley of pokeweed. That's all. Along the way was a tiny place still on today's maps called Aid; possibly aid was available there, but if so, the details of it were long ago lost.

There are only a few stories left to us from this early era of the Underground Railroad. One of them is about a man named Josephus. Josephus was enslaved by a Virginia ferryman who worked the river crossing to Marietta, Ohio. For whatever reason, Josephus chose not to run himself, but for at least twenty years, he spent many a night rowing fugitives across the river to Duck Creek on the Ohio side. The man who claimed ownership of Josephus never discovered his nocturnal activities; ironically, this Virginian did not consider Josephus to be very smart and constantly told him so. Josephus is said to have privately remarked that he seemed to get a lot smarter at night when his owner was not around. Additional facts about Josephus, including the years he was active, are not clear, but the lack of detail and general murkiness of the story suggest that it was early.[27]

Along this section of river in southeast Ohio, we can glean the names of about forty more African Americans who were station operators, but that number is both too high and too low.[28] Active dates for most of these people are missing, so some may not have appeared until midcentury. Conversely, there were surely many others who loosely participated in aiding freedom seekers in the early 1800s, but their names were never recorded and they are unknown to us now.

It is clear what many of the fugitives who reached this part of Ohio were fleeing. Straddling the Kanawha River near Charleston in western Virginia were the largest saltworks in the country. From about 1790, many enslaved workers labored there, much as Addison White had, but under large teams of coordinated overseers. Their experiences in the salt fields were no better than his, but for those brave and wily enough to follow it, the Kanawha flowed to the Ohio River and the region of free Black settlements beyond. An untold number of workers fled and found their way into Ohio down the Kanawha.

Farther downriver, after it takes its northward swing toward Cincinnati past that rounded hump, there lay another set of helpful settlements. Primary among these were the three Gist settlements in Brown, Adams and Highland Counties. These communities got their start in 1815 when the fabulously wealthy Englishman Samuel Gist, upon his death, freed all of his Virginia slaves. He owned hundreds, with a total value of several million dollars in today's money. Although we notice that he waited until his death to free the group, Gist was indeed well intentioned. For their long-term safety, he realized that these people would have to be removed from Virginia and transported to Ohio. Land would have to be acquired for them; moreover, funds would be needed for basic startup costs. Agricultural implements, seed, household goods and more had to be purchased; Gist also gave thought to the establishment of schools. Given a great deal of money to address all these needs, the executors of his will did what is all too familiar in our capitalist past. They absconded with most of it, although they did bring approximately three hundred newly freed people to Ohio and bought them some land. The rest of Gist's wishes were ignored. As a result, the people of the settlements struggled. Without employment opportunities as in Lawrence County, Gist residents were barely able to feed themselves at first. However, like the people of Poke Patch, they managed to scrape by for several decades before dispersing.[29]

The people of the Gist settlements may have had very little, but they were willing to share it with those escaping slavery. However, as years passed and the Underground Railroad developed to include more White people, Black communities like Gist faded somewhat in importance in the Underground Railroad. Slave catchers, also on the rise, saw the Black settlements as an obvious place to search for fugitives. Furthermore, under the Black Laws, the people of these communities had no recourse against whatever vicious aggression slave catchers inflicted on them. What did not change, however, was the settlements' helpful benefit of eliminating the novelty of dark skin. Because Black people lived in the area, a fugitive slave passing on a nearby road appeared to fit in and drew little notice.

The Gist story reveals the struggles faced by many of the Black settlements and how they nonetheless persevered to help themselves and others. But not all Black people who made it to Ohio suffered as much as the Gist residents. Some newcomers of color did quite well. One example is Jacob Gaskins, born to slavery in Winchester, Virginia. Freed when his master died, Gaskins accumulated enough money to relocate to the vicinity of Canton, Ohio, in 1817. Through hard work and skill, he increased his holdings to a well-tended farm of 375 acres. Much later, his farm was absorbed into a rambling golf course; modern-day men and women teeing off probably do not realize that the links are on the site of an Underground Railroad stop.[30]

Another successful newcomer to the state was Thomas C. Woodson. Born about 1790 in Virginia, Woodson managed to purchase freedom for himself and his wife, Jemima. They arrived in Chillicothe, Ohio, in 1820 but experienced it as inhospitable. Some writers would add the point that the town was founded and settled by Virginians, but that is only partly correct. Chillicothe fills a fertile loop of the Scioto River first peopled by Shawnee Indians decades before, but that is a story for another book. At any rate, the Woodsons were not fond of Chillicothe. Deciding to move to rural Jackson County, they organized a thriving community of about thirty families who together eventually owned two thousand acres. Woodson's portion of about four hundred acres was said to be the best farm in the county, and he was regarded as wealthy. The community, which he named Berlin Crossroads, was more successful than the other African American settlements previously mentioned. Berlin Crossroads participated in the Underground Railroad for many years, not deterred by an 1846 tragedy when Thomas Woodson Jr. was beaten to death by slave catchers for not revealing the location of a missing fugitive.[31]

Thomas and Jemima Woodson were both mixed-race, termed "mulattoes" in those days, and both believed themselves to have been fathered by their masters. Thomas Woodson Sr. seems to have been illiterate, but he was determined that his children be well educated. Berlin Crossroads included a quality school so highly regarded that some nearby White families enrolled their children as well. The Woodson children used the small school as a steppingstone to higher education. Each became prominent in his or her own right, helping to establish Ohio's Wilberforce University, among other achievements. Woodson's youngest daughter, Sarah, after graduating from Oberlin, was hired to teach at Wilberforce in 1858, becoming the first Black woman college professor in the nation and one of the very few female college instructors of any race. But possibly more interesting than Thomas Woodson's daughter is his father. Descendants maintain that Thomas Woodson was the son of Thomas Jefferson and Sally Hemings. She does seem to have given birth to a son called Tom close to 1790, but he is said to have died and been buried at Monticello. Clearly a cover story, say Woodson's descendants. They believe that he got out, assisted by excellent connections, and became the accomplished Thomas Woodson of Ohio. To date, DNA tests have neither proved nor disproved their belief.[32] Whoever his father and mother were, he and Gaskins are examples of the remarkable Black talent that found its way into Ohio during this era.

In focusing on these African Americans and the Black communities scattered about, we have bypassed the Quakers, who deserve a loud shout-out as early participants of the Underground Railroad. We floated right past them on our way down the Ohio but will now work our way back upriver. There were a few Quaker homes hewn from riverside forests as early as 1797; these were not lasting settlements, but at least one left evidence on our maps, that being Quaker Bottom in that lower tip of Lawrence County.[33] However, most of Ohio's earliest Quakers stopped before that point, coming ashore in Columbiana, Jefferson or Belmont County. After the founding in 1801 of Ohio's first monthly meeting in Belmont County, other meetinghouses followed. The influx then compounded as the burgeoning number of meetings drew even more Quakers to the area. An interesting side note is that several of the ministers of these early congregations were female. Additional Quaker communities later appeared in other parts of the state.

These Quakers, who had relocated from the upper South and Pennsylvania, held strong opinions on slavery. It is assumed that they offered assistance to fugitives as soon as their communities were established, although the amount of traffic they dealt with in the early years is unclear. The Quakers also collaborated with the residents of Guinea, a Belmont County African American community. This area's importance in the Underground Railroad never ceased into the 1860s; residents grew so confident that their antislavery viewpoint prevailed in the county that the Holloway brothers of Flushing even placed advertisements for their Underground Railroad station in the local newspaper.

The Underground Railroad in Ohio developed hand in hand with its population growth; the southern and eastern edges of Ohio—the areas in proximity to the river—were the first to offer some semblance of aid to fugitives. Northwest Ohio had few White or Black settlers until later and presents a much different story. The memoirs of Josiah Henson reveal the difference.[34] Josiah Henson was a very capable enslaved farm manager in Kentucky who earned an excellent income for his owner through his efficient management of agricultural operations. He had been promised freedom repeatedly, but the owner kept finding ways to renege. In the late summer of 1830, Henson and his wife, Charlotte, finally decided to flee with their four young children in tow. Using a needle and thread and the heaviest fabric she could find, Charlotte Henson fashioned a baby carrier that held not one child but two. It was for their two youngest children—and also for Josiah, who would tote them for the duration of the journey. The family even rehearsed before they fled, making sure that her handiwork balanced comfortably and held up against wiggles. Then, one moonless night in the middle of September, the strange ensemble walked to the banks of the Ohio River not far from their western Kentucky residence. Josiah had prepared for the crossing, and a boat awaited. The group then set out north and east across Indiana. Josiah wore the baby device as Charlotte coaxed along a third child; only their oldest was self-sufficient and even able to help.

Already carrying the children, they were limited in the amount of food they could bring. Henson's memoirs mention no food other than beef jerky and no Underground Railroad stations encountered in Indiana. However, they had chosen the right time of year to flee, when the land itself offered some sustenance. If there were White settlements, there were cornfields—an excellent food source in early fall when the kernels were still soft and chewable. Later on, the corn would be rock hard and require grinding. Agricultural development also suggested that there would be squashes and pumpkins in gardens and apples on trees. Henson does not mention it, but some fugitives pilfered livestock; one described smothering a pig in a way that prevented it from squealing and alerting the farmer. Sometimes fires and cooking were

Josiah Henson walked with his young family to Canada in 1830. *New York Public Library.*

presumed safe; at other times, meat was consumed raw.[35] Tidy farms or no, there would have been nuts in the woods. Like many other fugitives before and after, the Hensons knew that fall was their friend. It offered many advantages: fewer rains than in spring, less mud to slow them and leave tracks. More foliage for camouflage. Various food sources, especially those straight tall rows of edible corn. A person could sit in a cornfield and eat undetected for hours before safely nodding off for the night. Through September and into October, the Hensons were able to piece together a meager diet, although everyone must have gotten hungry as the days wore on. Late in the two-week trek to Cincinnati, Josiah took the chance of buying some food at a farmhouse—a fortuitous transaction, although selling food does not qualify a home as an Underground Railroad station.

The Hensons rested in Cincinnati for the next two weeks, where they were well cared for. With a Black population of several thousand and an established Quaker congregation, there was no shortage of households in the city offering generous room and board. But if the Hensons were to reach Canada before bad weather set in, they could not tarry long. The family headed north on an old military road that had been laid through the wilderness of western Ohio during the War of 1812. They walked and walked. This was mostly wild country, with no fields under cultivation; hunger was even worse here. Had they been in eastern Ohio, a wealth of Black and Quaker households would have offered them aid; here there was only nature. Josiah seems not to have anticipated this, a rare hole in his careful planning. He was not prepared to be a hunter-gatherer, nor did he have the time for it. They had to keep walking. At one point, Charlotte Henson fainted from hunger. Flirting with disaster, the family finally chanced on a band of Indians—probably Wyandots. Each group was utterly charmed by the other, the Indians being particularly taken with the small, dark babies. That fascination, coupled with their basic generosity, moved the Indians to feed and shelter the Hensons. Josiah Henson admired the wisdom and calm judgment of the group's chief; he treated them well, without the silly antics some of the tribe engaged in with the Henson children. The Indians communicated that the "big lake" was not far away; a few of the young tribesmen accompanied the family part of the distance to make sure they took the correct path. The family easily reached the Lake Erie port town of Sandusky to find that the ships were still running; it was not yet November, and the weather remained fair. Passage was arranged with a helpful captain, and all six Hensons made it safely to Canada.

There are two points to note in Josiah Henson's story. The first is a reminder never to equate literacy with intelligence. Josiah is one of several people in this book who was clearly bright, although life had not afforded him the opportunity to read. To succeed, he was required to remember and synthesize information without referring to text. He had directed planting, harvesting and animal care at multiple locations—his owner's fields stretched on for miles. He planned how to get his family of six to Canada and afterward eloquently dictated a detailed account of it. He also served as a Methodist minister, reciting his favorite scriptures from memory while preaching. Josiah had plenty of smarts and probably recognized a similar nonliterate form of intelligence in the Indian chief he had admired. Later in his life in Canada, he finally did learn to read, but he had previously managed very well without that skill.

The second point of interest is the presence of Indian tribes in the Underground Railroad. Since it involved the interactions of not one but *two* groups that normally lacked literacy, scholars have had difficulty recovering this story. Neither the enslaved nor the Indians left much in the way of written records. But we have a sufficient number of hints, such as their presence in Josiah Henson's memoirs, to suspect that Indians routinely gave aid. The Ottawa village on the Maumee River presided over by Chief Kinjeino (near present-day Toledo) was a documented aid station for fugitives, as was Ottawa chief Ocquenisie's town on the Blanchard River to its south. Pottawatomie and Shawnee Indians are said to have helped freedom seekers at Chief Winameg's village near the Michigan border and at the present-day town of Wapakoneta, respectively. In fact, there may have been a better aid system in these areas when populated with Indians than in the following period when White people had replaced them. And beyond here, in the still wild areas of Indiana and Michigan, it is certain that Underground Railroad travelers received help from natives.[36]

The story of Indians in the Underground Railroad has long been buried, but it makes sense. Catty-cornered across from the early settlements of southeast Ohio, this swampy land comprised the last corner of the state to gain a nonnative population. Up to 1830, Indians were the primary population group in northwest Ohio. By treaty they were still allowed to be there; stated another way, this land had not yet been taken from them. The port of Sandusky, where many freedom seekers disembarked for Canada, was not far from lands controlled by the Ottawas and Wyandots. It is only logical that fugitives encountered them en route. A tiny twist in this story is that after spending a night or two with the Indians, some chose not to disembark at all.

The Pottawatomies and other Indians aided freedom seekers passing through northwest Ohio. *Library of Congress.*

There are known instances of escaping Blacks choosing to remain in these secluded communities and adapt to native society. The Blacks and Indians had no reason for hostilities. After all, these dark people had not come intending to settle on Indian land; most were just passing through. Why not feed them and encourage their continued journey? Besides, united by their well-deserved distrust of "palefaces," the two population groups generally seemed to get along; in some locations, there was evidence of intermarriage and mention of "Black Indians."

Indian tribes constitute an unappreciated part of the Underground Railroad. They may not be a large part of that story, but they certainly deserve a mention in its early chapters. It appears that the Hensons would not have reached Canada without help from the Indians, and this assistance was probably crucial to other travelers as well. The others just did not leave memoirs as Josiah Henson did.

Chapter 4

OHIO AND THE NATION, 1815–1860

With the War of 1812 won and stability ensured, our new nation entered into a period of significant growth and development. Primary examples were transportation improvements that facilitated travel to faraway portions of the country. These would have a major effect on Ohio and the Underground Railroad.

Going down a river like the Ohio had always been easy. But how to come back up? River-based trade was limited until this problem was solved. A young Ohioan named Richard Elson five times in his life built a flatboat to take agricultural goods all the way to New Orleans. Once there, he disassembled the boat, sold its wood and walked the thousand miles back to his Stark County home. Five times. We know about Elson because he witnessed the worst of slavery on his trips and subsequently became active in the Underground Railroad.[37] His story illustrates the shortcomings of river commerce in the early days. Flatboats and rafts, not just a literary device in works by Mark Twain, were commonplace on the Mississippi. But they could only go one way. Once you reached the delta, you were going to walk from there, whether it was "to light out for the territory" like Huckleberry Finn or walk back to Ohio like Richard Elson.

Elson presumably returned north on the Natchez Trace, a path trod for centuries by Indians. By the 1800s, it had become an actual road wide enough to accommodate wagons. Its chief advantage was its arrow-straight route from Natchez, Mississippi, all the way to Maysville, Kentucky, and the banks of the Ohio, cutting off miles from the meandering path of the unhurried

Mississippi. At the same time, a caveat was that any ruffian or tough living nearby knew that the industrious-looking fellows heading northward were nearly always carrying a recently earned profit. The unlucky and foolhardy among them were regularly relieved of the burden of their coins; they then faced a long walk home from a fruitless journey.

Robert Fulton eventually responded to the problem of one-way river travel, and by 1815, a group of hardy steam-driven paddle boats were plying their way down—and up!—the Mississippi and the Ohio. Suddenly Maysville mattered less and Cincinnati boomed, becoming the fastest-growing city in the United States.

In the same decade, canals added to the array of navigable waterways. The first segment of the Erie Canal opened in 1817; by 1825, it was delivering masses of travelers and goods across New York. From its end near Buffalo, there remained only an easy jaunt across Lake Erie to Ohio's northern border. This new canal was one reason why so many people from the Northeast settled in northern Ohio, coloring its political leanings to this day. Ohio voting maps reveal an enduring electoral chasm between its lakeside counties and the southern-oriented population living closer to the Ohio River.

Ohio statesmen and entrepreneurs, envious of the huge success of the Erie Canal, wanted canals of their own; they embarked on the construction of two main ones, each stretching from the Ohio River to Lake Erie. The first, completed in 1832, ran along the course of the Scioto River in central Ohio before taking a northeasterly path to Cleveland. The second soon followed, facilitated by the Miami River out of Cincinnati and ending at Toledo on the western end of the lake. Unlike the Mohawk Valley in New York, a relatively flat and easy place for a canal, Ohio posed an elevation gain across its middle, requiring a significant number of costly locks. While neither could match New York's Erie Canal for financial windfall, Ohio's canals, including all their extensions and feeders, were nonetheless temporarily important for commerce and for the Underground Railroad.

The speed of canal travel and the speed of traveling *upstream* on one of the early sternwheelers were about the same: four miles per hour. Unlike the riverboats, the canalboats, pulled by mules, went this same steady rate northward or southward. They traveled only in daylight; plus, added time needed to be factored in to traverse the series of locks, so it could take two or three weeks to cover the entire length of one of Ohio's canals. Nonetheless, for travelers who had previously endured bumpy wagons and creaking carriages, the canalboats offered a blessedly placid ride and were considered a wonder—for a short time.

Ohio's canals provided new travel options in the 1820s. *Library of Congress.*

Canal development was driven by investors buying stock. *Ed Schulz.*

Before the second of Ohio's canals was even completed, a better transportation option came into play: railroads. Now the state needed to build railroads, the newest marvel of the age. Trains were noisy and impressive and went so much faster; the whole populace of the country began clamoring for them. In the late 1830s, railroads were introduced in Ohio, and words like *conductor, station, transfer* and *depot* came into common use. An enthralled population learned that travel could be speedy and grew accustomed to the idea of touring about.

As transportation patterns in the country shifted, so too did the places where agricultural products were grown and the means by which they were taken to market. River trade boosted Louisiana's profits from sugarcane, but the major commodity affected was cotton. The cotton gin had already increased the cotton business, so much so that the lands where cotton had first been grown could not keep up. Fertility was declining. Beginning in about 1815, cotton growers started to move west into Alabama, Mississippi and Arkansas. By the mid-1830s, those three areas were dominating cotton output,[38] and all had achieved statehood. Efficient travel on the Mississippi was a large factor in this development.

All the new cotton fields in proximity to the Mississippi triggered further momentous change. This effect occurred upriver and is disturbing to ponder. More and more workers were needed in the huge cotton fields, with escalating prices paid for labor. In Alabama and Mississippi, the slave populations exploded, increasing sixfold between 1820 and 1840.[39] Considering how

Transportation improvements of the nineteenth century aided freedom seekers. *Ohio History Connection.*

hard these enslaved people were forced to work, it is ridiculous to suppose that this growth resulted from births among the workforce. The people, of course, were brought in. Not from Africa, because laws had shut that trade down in 1807. Where could new workers be found? The obvious place was right up the river in the conveniently located state of Kentucky. Whoever coined the phrase "to be sold down the river" was surely a Kentuckian.

The green hills of Kentucky rest on limestone—formed by the same forces that produced the salt licks. Calcium from the limestone finds its way into the area's unique bluegrass, providing an excellent diet for horses, nourishing their long, strong bones. Crystal clear streams flow out of the limestone hills with water that is perfect for whiskey distillers. But how many slaves does it take to groom and feed some horses or distill and age bourbon? Not many at all compared to the number needed for growing and picking an acre of cotton.

Moreover, a typical slaveholder of Kentucky had a small farm nestled in between hills with just a few workers. In such a location, a single dark-skinned family might be serving a White one. No one will ever suggest that slavery was in any way acceptable, but the slave experience in the "hollers" was slightly more salubrious than in some other environments. Many enslaved people in a border state like Kentucky experienced reasonable work assignments and adequate diets; they were able to mate and have babies at normal rates. The problem was that these babies were not necessarily needed as workers in Kentucky—they were needed elsewhere.

In an earlier era, many slave owners of the Tidewater region had thought it unseemly and unnecessary to break up slave families. That viewpoint was now sadly absent. Slave families were broken up with abandon to get more workers into the expanding cotton fields of the Deep South, where they sold for about 40 percent more than in Virginia or Kentucky.[40] By the 1840s, slaves in Kentucky did not just produce its agricultural goods. Much more appalling, the slaves *themselves* were regarded as a major product of the state, similar to Thoroughbreds, hemp, whiskey, salt and tobacco.

Kentuckians took to slave trading with zeal. In the early days, little coinage or scrip existed on the frontier, making barter the expected means of exchange. Kentucky folks grew used to bartering for just about everything—horse trading, for example. They often bartered slaves for land so that slaves became a strange type of living currency. The Kentucky propensity for slave trading showed up far beyond the Bluegrass; as early as 1800, 80 percent of transactions in the busy Natchez, Mississippi market involved Kentuckians.[41]

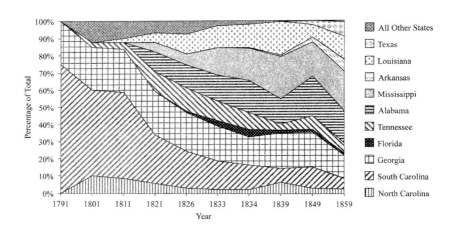

Moving westward: Production of cotton by U.S. states, 1790–1860

Cotton production shifted west, affecting residents of the upper Mississippi watershed. Sven Beckert.

It takes only a brief glance at a United States map to predict the effect of these pressures. The westward swing of cotton cultivation forced many enslaved people down the Mississippi, a history unwittingly revealed in Kentucky's popular state song.[42] However, it also increased *fugitive* traffic heading in the opposite direction through the Mississippi watershed and across the Ohio. By the midpoint of the nineteenth century, these northward escapes had ballooned. The pattern was particularly worrisome for Indiana and Illinois. Motivated by the same fears that inspired Ohio's Black Laws, these free states, established thirty-some years before, both wrote "anti-Negro" provisions directly into revised midcentury constitutions.[43] Fifty years into its own statehood, Ohio similarly addressed general growth issues with a constitutional revision but avoided tampering with the basic doctrine of race neutrality. Instead, and unlike its neighbors to the west, by 1850 Ohio was improving justice for residents of color, having recently repealed its most egregious racial laws.

Across the river from all three states was Kentucky. Unlike Addison White, many of the migrants were not fleeing Kentucky as much as they were escaping the inevitable pull into the Deep South. Reverend Rankin in Ripley was one Underground Railroad operator who routinely asked new arrivals their reasons for fleeing. He often heard responses like, "My master was not so mean, but he's old…he's sick…he's in financial trouble…it looks like he will sell out…he would have sold me." Some variation of this theme was particularly common among family groups who fled together. They knew that they had to get out of Kentucky to protect their nuclear family unit—and to stay out of cotton fields.[44]

This is not meant to imply that all slaves in Kentucky had a tolerable life. Counter to that notion is the example of Margaret Garner. You already know about Garner if you are aware of Ohio native Toni Morrison's novel *Beloved* or saw the related movie or opera. Margaret Garner was a Kentucky woman who managed to reach Cincinnati with her husband and four children, all enslaved, in 1856. Unfortunately, slave catchers caught the group, and during the melee that followed, Margaret Garner killed her two-year-old daughter with a kitchen knife rather than allow her to be taken back into slavery. Indeed, Garner was preparing to kill more of her brood and herself as well but was prevented from doing so.

The sexual services demanded of Margaret Garner were what made slavery unendurable for her. Garner was mixed-race, thought to be the daughter of her mother's owner. Some of her own four children were even lighter skinned, likely the offspring of a later owner of the plantation. In the story left to us, her focus during the horrible event was on her daughters, less so on her sons. After her arrest, Garner was taken to trial

It is often forgotten that Stephen Foster was describing Kentuckians "sold down the river" in this 1853 song. *Author's collection.*

100 DOLLARS

REWARD!

Ranaway from the subscriber on the 27th of July, my Black Woman, named

EMILY,

Seventeen years of age, well grown, black color, has a whining voice. She took with her one dark calico and one blue and white dress, a red corded gingham bonnet; a white striped shawl and slippers. I will pay the above reward if taken near the Ohio river on the Kentucky side, or THREE HUNDRED DOLLARS, if taken in the State of Ohio, and delivered to me near Lewisburg, Mason County, Ky.   THO'S. H. WILLIAMS.
August 4, 1853.

Left: Sales "down the river" and the breakup of families caused many slaves to flee. *Ohio History Connection*.

Opposite: Northerners became increasingly alarmed about the evils of slavery. *Library of Congress.*

in Cincinnati; a preliminary legal question was whether to charge her as a human being who had killed another human being or whether to regard her as property that had destroyed property. Jockeying back and forth on this issue went on for weeks. Her defense attorneys pushed for a murder charge; there were many good reasons for this, including the fact that they anticipated a governor's pardon in the event of a guilty verdict. These events occurred one summer before the Addison White affair; the Garner trial can be seen as a prelude to the next big one, both provoking rowdy crowds that milled around the courthouse for days. In the end, she was not tried for murder and was simply returned to her owner. There is no way to sugarcoat this story, and it has no happy ending. Margaret Garner was sent to Arkansas, where she died in 1858.[45]

The past few paragraphs are abhorrent, but something positive grew out of the awful aspects of slavery. This same information you just read was read contemporaneously by people of the nineteenth century, causing antislavery attitudes to surge in the North. Moreover, now linked through an improved north–south transportation system, northerners did not just read about slavery; many traveled into the South and witnessed it firsthand. By the 1840s, much of the northern populace, who in 1820 might not have bothered to take a position on slavery, had become incensed by it. The North was increasingly energized, and more and more people identified with the antislavery movement.

Another important development was happening specifically in Ohio. As the population of the country shifted rapidly west, the country's academics

Union with Freemen--No Union with Slaveholders.

ANTI-SLAVERY
MEETINGS!

Anti-Slavery Meetings will be held in this place, to commence on   at
in the

To be Addressed by

Agents of the Western ANTI-SLAVERY SOCIETY.

Three millions of your fellow beings are in chains--the Church and Government sustains the horrible system of oppression.

Turn Out!

AND LEARN YOUR DUTY TO YOURSELVES, THE SLAVE AND GOD.

EMANCIPATION or DISSOLUTION, and a FREE NORTHERN REPUBLIC!

HOMESTEAD PRINT, SALEM, OHIO.

realized that educational institutions could not continue to solely hug the East Coast. Across the Alleghenies, whole new generations of youth were growing up, and towns needed teachers and preachers. Education had to be offered in proximity to these needs. Thus, just about every religious denomination that existed established a college or seminary for young men of the "West," which usually meant in Ohio. Most of these institutions fostered progressive, antislavery thought; some would directly impact the Underground Railroad.

Up to this point, the word *abolitionist* has barely appeared on these pages, as it can only be used with explanation and care. Many people of the North had antislavery views, but only a few of these called themselves abolitionists. Antislavery people disliked the horrid institution but pondered various ways to end it, many of them gradual. How would freed slaves support themselves? Where would they go—could this be back to Africa? Should slave owners be reimbursed for their financial losses? Wouldn't it be better to manage slavery in such a way as to make it die out over time? To all these questions, abolitionists answered, "Hogwash! Slavery is an evil, ungodly institution that should be ended immediately. Without all this stalling. Now." Only a small portion of antislavery thinkers initially took this position, which was generally seen as an extreme, radical view.

Abolitionist, often used as a pejorative, was a word meant to scare people, and it did. So even though antislavery sentiment was growing, we will still generally stick to that compound word and avoid using *abolitionist* except for a few known cases. Certain writers in Northeast newspapers were abolitionists. John Brown (of Ohio) was an abolitionist, Frederick Douglass was an abolitionist and Reverend Rankin was an abolitionist. Many other northern Whites, even many of the people assisting the Underground Railroad, were not. In the late 1850s, Abraham Lincoln began speaking and writing forcefully against slavery, and yet even he would not have called himself an abolitionist. Not yet.

The last decade before the Civil War constitutes the last gasp of peaceful coexistence of North and South. The nation was trapped in a dangerous vortex, a downward spiral of dissenting views. The 1850 Fugitive Slave Law, requiring all northerners to function as slave catchers on command, was the beginning of the end. Northern Blacks had been subject to various Black Laws for some time, but this 1850 federal law affected White people—and aroused their anger. The status of slavery in western states, which had been teetering back and forth for decades, caused further outrage that could no longer be tamped down through compromise. The Dred Scott decision in the spring of 1857 reduced the chances of a peaceful resolution. The Supreme Court decision was not written narrowly but rather expansively; Chief Justice Taney declared not only that Dred Scott was a slave and always would be a slave regardless of where he resided, but also that no resident of African descent could *ever* have the rights of a U.S. citizen. Furthermore, Taney maintained that all areas of the United States and its territories had the right to entertain slavery if they so chose. This meant that the Northwest Ordinance of 1787, which had disallowed slavery in the whole region, was retroactively invalid. Southerners cheered the decade's laws for favoring their point of view, but in effect, the legal overreach sped up the collision course the nation was on, hurling it toward civil war. Kansas, where people were openly shooting each other, was already there.

Southerners may have gained some legal opinions that tilted in their favor in the 1850s, but northerners got something even more influential. They got a book that regular folks could easily read and understand. Harriet Beecher Stowe's *Uncle Tom's Cabin* was published to immediate acclaim in 1852. Stowe seemed to prove that not only was the pen mightier than the sword, it was also more powerful than judicial scales and dense legal text. Inspired by events and stories Stowe had picked up during her extended stay in Ohio, the bestseller was eye-opening to many northerners. It swung public opinion in the North hard to the antislavery side.

The momentous decade of the 1850s ended with abolitionist John Brown's 1859 raid on Harpers Ferry; this incident and its aftermath dwarfed all previously mentioned events in importance to the frayed American public. It was debated then and now whether Brown was a brave and glorious hero or a madman—no one knows. It is easier to agree that this may have been the de facto start of the Civil War. As Brown himself believed, bloodshed would be required to eradicate slavery from the nation.

Chapter 5

GETTING TO OHIO

To use the Underground Railroad, the enslaved first had to reach it—no easy endeavor. Very few accomplished this feat from a great distance. Those who came from as far as Tennessee braved a meticulously planned, weeks-long journey that required cunning and perseverance. This accomplishment was not the norm.[46] Most freedom seekers entered Ohio after a much shorter journey. Leaving aside travel on boats, land-based travel on the Underground Railroad generally came out of a narrow band bordering the Mason-Dixon line and the Ohio River. Only in northerly parts of Maryland, Virginia and Kentucky did enslaved people even hear about the Underground Railroad, making it a viable option of escape. Except for port cities, the Underground Railroad was unknown in the Deep South.

If we could watch a time-condensed depiction of the Underground Railroad from fifty thousand feet above, we would mostly see a small bleed out from the upper edge of the slave states, along with a few boats moving up the Mississippi or along the Atlantic coast. The movements would be sparse in the early years but get denser over time. The largest portion of all the land travel would move directly into Ohio.

Ohio's station keepers aided any freedom seeker who came to them, but it was extremely rare for agents to journey into a slave state to assist there. The incomparable Harriet Tubman is the well-known exception, traveling multiple times deep into eastern Maryland with a loaded gun in her petite dress pocket. A cadre of Ohio Valley agents that can be counted on one hand similarly ventured into slave territory on impressive missions. All of them were African Americans, and most had once been enslaved. One was John Parker, whose achievements will be described later. Another was Indiana-based Elijah Anderson, who often brought large groups of slaves through Ohio to a Lake Erie port on journeys that had usually originated deep inside Kentucky. Anderson was highly effective and respected by antislavery colleagues, although he was eventually caught in Kentucky, likely due to a tip from an acquaintance eager to collect the bounty Kentucky had placed on his head.[47] But the roaming agent with the most interesting modus operandi was Richard Naylor of Martin's Ferry, Ohio, just across the river from Wheeling. Naylor would cross the river to meet with the enslaved, advising them about escape methods and giving specific details on destinations, even recruiting them for flight. Then he would proceed to get very drunk. White folks in Wheeling and around the Virginia Panhandle regarded him as amusing and harmless—just another town drunk. It has never been clear if Naylor was hopelessly addicted to alcohol or if his drinking was primarily a ruse. Either way, he was effective for years until someone got wise, prompting him to relocate to Canada.[48]

A few White residents scattered throughout the upper South worked against slavery and aided freedom seekers, but without collaborators or routes, they existed beyond the actual Underground Railroad. While it would take an encyclopedia to list all their counterparts in Ohio, these known examples of the South are few enough to be individually named. The most daring and inventive was John Fairfield.[49] Born to a large Virginia plantation and in line to inherit scores of slaves, Fairfield had the insight to detest the "peculiar institution" and spent his adult life undercutting it one way or another. The first slave he liberated was his childhood playmate Bill, followed by others owned by his relatives. An uncle tried to have his nephew arrested; the young man responded by changing his name and moving about—he also used other confusing aliases but is identified today as John Fairfield. He traveled throughout the upper South, normally accompanied by one or two "slaves" whom he addressed harshly in public. These African American men were able to convey the group's true mission of liberation to the enslaved community while Fairfield engaged with Whites. He often posed as a poultry dealer, but his favorite ploy was to present himself as a slave trader gathering groups of people to sell down the river. With a complicated financial agreement that never quite materialized, the duped slave owners did not realize that their "property" was headed north across the Ohio, not down it. Fairfield particularly focused on reuniting families who had splintered when some had made it to freedom but others had been left behind.

Fairfield was often in Ohio conducting freedom seekers, sometimes accompanying them all the way to Canada from Ashtabula Harbor. He was known to lodge occasionally with Levi Coffin in Cincinnati or with Reverend Rankin in Ripley. Both were dismayed by his exploits and bizarre risks but remained his friends. Stories abound about Fairfield, mostly true but some apocryphal; the tale that he faked a funeral, with a solemn procession of African Americans walking behind an open casket and one of their own playing the part of the deceased, is probably in the latter category. Those who tell it claim that White Kentuckians respectfully stepped aside and thought nothing of it when the group boarded boats for a Negro cemetery in Cincinnati.

Probably an embroidered version of events that took place elsewhere, this incident is at least in the spirit of what Fairfield would do. His ruses and schemes could be amazingly complex. He may have played this to the end—or the presumed end. He is thought to have been attacked and killed while working a scam in Tennessee; however, there is evidence that he faked this death in order to escape to the West. Someone with his exact name, age and birthplace turns up in the 1860 census in Kansas Territory, a Free State battleground that would have suited him.[50]

A few other committed, if less colorful, people of the South worked against slavery, some highly influenced by time spent in Ohio. Oberlin College had an impact far beyond its northern Ohio location. Kentuckian John Fee, known to advise fleeing slaves, had studied there and returned to establish the town of Berea and its progressive college modeled on Oberlin. The fascinating Vermont-born Delia Webster also studied at Oberlin before moving to Kentucky to teach and fight slavery. She eventually bought a farm along the Ohio River and assisted slave journeys, often working with her friend Reverend Calvin Fairbank, who had likewise relocated to Kentucky from the North. They sometimes brought people far upriver to the safe haven of Ripley.

It was the lucky freedom seeker who encountered one of these brave southern abolitionists. In the great majority of cases, help like this did not exist in slave states; escapees had to independently figure out how to get north. Only then, when fugitives entered a free state like Ohio, did they reach the Underground Railroad. It existed only in free states as a means of moving people farther north to assured safety; this usually, though not always, meant Canada.

One of the myths of the Underground Railroad relates to this northward travel. It is common to think of these travelers humming the "Follow the

Drinking Gourd" song that kept them pointed in the direction of the North Star. In reality, people of that day knew the night sky better than we do and did not need any song to remind them of it. Moreover, that particular song was probably not written until very late in the antebellum period. It is one of a number of folk beliefs and symbols that honor the Underground Railroad after the fact more than they were used in it. Harriet Tubman described singing to her passengers to alert them that it was time to move, but she did not use the drinking gourd song.[51] Regardless, these and other symbols have acquired deep meaning in recalling that era. Today's populace, including children, eagerly learn about the Underground Railroad through this folklore, which does no harm. The thoughtful person has to be careful, however, in accepting all of it as historically accurate.

The Ohio River may have been a beckoning symbol of the freedom beyond, but it was also a barrier to it. To reach the Underground Railroad in Ohio, one had to cross this river; the time of year determined one's options. The simplest way was to walk across, as one could do most winters. Station operators in river towns knew to expect "guests" on the coldest nights of January or February. Surprisingly, there are also a few accounts of the river being shallow enough to wade at the tail end of some dry summers. The advantages of ripe food and abundant foliage in August and September are easily imagined; this added benefit is less expected. It may be hard to credit these tales now, but there was more seasonal variability of river depths before the dams, levees and various forms of control provided by today's U.S. Army Corps of Engineers. In addition, the canal system exacerbated occasional low water. As often as possible, canals were well-maintained channels in preexisting rivers, but in some places, whole new water courses had been dug. One can create a new channel but not the water to go in it, which had to come from nature's existing hydrology system. There was only so much water to go around; water cannot just be conjured up.[52]

In the months when the river was not frozen, one way to get across was to swim. Fit men like Addison White could manage it, but swimming was not an option for most women or children. Tice Davids was another who swam it, achieving both freedom and notoriety. In 1831, Davids was fleeing Kentucky just steps ahead of his owner; fortunately, he could swim and got across the river while the White man searched for a boat. The owner felt sure he could spot the wet Davids in Ripley but never did. Befuddled, he later said that it was "as if the slave had gone off on some underground road."[53] The incident was picked up in the press, where the wording evolved into "Underground Railroad." Railroads being the new thing of the day, much as the information revolution was to our generation, railroad terminology was inventively applied to the fugitive system.

If one could not walk, wade or swim the river, that left boats. A lucky few of the enslaved did work such as produce delivery that allowed them to routinely row across the river without suspicion.[54] But for most, canoes or skiffs had to be "borrowed" in the dark of night for the purpose of crossing; however, this seems to have grown more difficult as the years wore on. On the Ohio side of the river, boats might be casually strewn about as was convenient, but this was rarely the case on the Kentucky side, where care was taken to padlock boats and remove oars. Ohioans were not likely to be looking for a boat to sneak into Kentucky, but a steady stream of Kentucky folk wanted to slip silently into Ohio.

Fugitives had to search diligently for a free boat plus oars, or else they had to enlist help. We have already learned about Josephus, who ferried fugitives across the river for a few decades in the vicinity of Marietta; others offered the service at additional ports. A fascinating African American woman was linked to a covert transport between Belpre, Ohio and Parkersburg, (West) Virginia. It is not clear whether "Aunt Jenny" was enslaved or free; regardless, she had the job of operating Parkersburg's warning horn on foggy nights. Throughout the night, Jenny was to frequently blow the foghorn, which sounded across the shoals bordering the city. She was reliable in the work and even sounded the horn at other times as well, which no one seemed to mind. These errant soundings actually alerted Underground Railroad operative John Stone across the river that fugitives were waiting in her small cabin. Stone would arrange to have them ferried across and assist with their further journey. Parkersburg to Belpre was a popular crossing point for both enslaved and free people due to the road system; the State of Virginia had built important turnpikes running from Alexandria to Staunton and then all the way to Parkersburg. Fugitives may not have openly traveled on it, but if they at least kept the turnpike in sight, they could track their way across the confusing Appalachians. Stone and Jenny moved a lot of people without interacting in person. He may or may not have known that "Aunt Jenny" was a code name and that her real name was Edna Sutton. When freedom came, Ms. Sutton moved to Ohio, where she initially supported herself working on a railroad crew, disguised as a man named Ed Sutton. She was one of the many cunning and innovative people of the Underground Railroad.[55]

Arnold Cragston, enslaved for the first twenty-five years of his life, provided a similar ferry service between Maysville and Ripley. He was allowed to regularly go out "courtin'"—allowances for such activity must be made. One night, he heard that a strong rower was needed to get a young girl across the river. Initially reluctant to get involved, he later decided to comply because she was so pretty. Of course, it could be no lasting relationship due to his return to Kentucky, but he continued rowing groups across on the darkest nights for many months afterward. It was only later that he resettled to Indiana.[56] Farther downriver, a riverside shack purported to be a fishing business; in reality, it was headquarters for yet another secret ferry service.[57] Undoubtedly, additional ferrying occurred in a variety of locations, most of it of the ad hoc variety. Because most locations lacked foghorns like Aunt Jenny's, the hoot owl signal was a common call across the river to request a pickup. In other places, a lantern signal was utilized.[58]

There was yet another way to cross—the most difficult of all. But you would only do it if you were desperate, as was the woman who accomplished it; she had heard her owner speak of selling slaves and feared being separated from her young son. On a late winter night in 1838, this mother ran, carrying her child, who may have been as old as two, from her Kentucky home to the Ohio River a few miles away. She briefly rested in the shoreside cabin of a kindly older man, who advised her that she would be crazy to go out on the ice that night because it was breaking up. But he could not deter her, so he gave her a long fence rail that he thought might assist.

On the Ohio side, families like the Parkers and Rankins were sleeping soundly, certain that no one could traverse the river under breakup conditions. Only a lone slave catcher named Chancey Shaw was out, for reasons of his own, walking along the riverbank, and it was he who documented what occurred. The woman did cross, jumping and crawling across the ice floes. More than once she hoisted her son to the next ice block and had to then pull herself up out of the water onto it. The rail saved her at times, but balancing toddler plus timber could not have been easy. Shaw watched, dumbfounded, as she finally reached the Ohio shore. Normally, this would have represented easy money for him, but he had lost interest in financial gain. Instead, he helped her up the riverbank and pointed to Reverend Rankin's house up the hill. In effect, he said, "Go on up there and they will help you. Anyone who made it across that ice tonight deserves freedom."

She let herself into the quiet Rankin home, its door always unlocked. Sometime later, one of the family awoke to find her silently sitting in front of the warm hearth tending her child. The Rankins at first did not believe her story of crossing the ice, thinking it impossible. But Shaw later confirmed her achievement; moreover, her shawl was found dropped on the riverbank. If the Rankins got her name before sending her north to

Harriet Beecher Stowe based the story of Eliza crossing dangerous ice on a true incident. *Library of Congress.*

Canada, they did not record it. However, they later described the incident to houseguest Harriet Beecher Stowe, who memorialized the story in *Uncle Tom's Cabin*, naming her Eliza Harris.

The coda of the Eliza story is her surprising return. Three years later, Eliza left her son in safe hands in Canada and, on a summer day, approached the Rankin home. She was accompanied by a French Canadian man in her employ. Their plan was to cross into Kentucky to retrieve additional loved ones stranded in slavery. In her book, Stowe and her illustrators fashioned Eliza into a pretty new mother barely out of girlhood; actually, Eliza was a stocky mixed-race woman a few decades older than the fictional character. Still in Kentucky were other children and even grandchildren, some fathered by an overseer. Eliza had told the Rankins that she would come back; still, they were appalled by her dangerous proposal and begged her to reconsider. Once again the intrepid woman could not be deterred, and once again she succeeded; this time, several helpful townspeople of Ripley played roles in getting her young family to safety.[59]

Eliza's river crossing abilities are matched by no one, and her winter method is definitely not recommended. Her heroic story introduces a category of character from the other end of river society: the slave catcher. Slave catchers were not admired by anyone; slave owners may have relied on them, but even they tended to look down on those who dealt in this unsavory and often dishonest trade. Slave catchers were generally considered the dregs of society. Only rarely did a slave catcher work a specific case like a detective, hired by a slave owner to go after a particular escapee. Occasionally, they looked for fugitives who had appeared in runaway ads. But most of the time slave catchers were self-employed and did what we would consider wholesale work. They simply roamed around searching for anyone who looked like an escaped slave and picked them up. Many of the apprehended individuals had free status, although that did little to impress the slave catchers. If freedom papers were produced, and most of the time they could not be, the documents were disregarded.

There are records of slave catchers harassing Ohio's free Blacks, with retaliation from local White citizens, going back to at least 1806.[60]

Slave catchers, most of whom were Kentuckians, needed to trade in volume to make money; the economics of the single "returned slave" did not serve them well. A slave who had run away had reduced value—a "runner" was thought to always be a "runner." Besides, a returning runaway could pass ideas and route information on to others. For this reason, owners did not pursue fleeing slaves with much vigor, only occasionally bothering to place ads for their return and offer reward money. Most fugitives had more to fear from unknown slave catchers than from their alleged owners. In the 1840s and 1850s, the numbers of slave catchers increased along with the numbers of freedom seekers.[61]

Whoever a slave catcher captured in Ohio was taken to an auction block in Kentucky or Virginia. For the economics to work out in the slave catcher's favor, he needed to produce a group of people, the value of an apprehended fugitive now reduced to about three-fourths of what it otherwise would have been. Slave catchers did not mind the discounted price; if they worked in

A BOLD STROKE FOR FREEDOM.

Slave catchers were a rough crowd, but some freedom seekers were armed. *Library of Congress.*

volume, they could still make a profit. There was a good market for these people farther south. From the point of view of the slave-owning world, the best option was to sell "runners" down the river. Far away in the cotton fields, the "problems" of a past runaway were not going to make much difference.

Slave catchers may have been an uneducated lot, but they were not stupid. They frequented areas that freedom seekers had to pass through. Some resorted to trickery, enticing slaves to bolt, only to capture and resell them. These dangerous lowlifes flocked to the counties near the Ohio River; another group plied the state's northern edge near Lake Erie ports. Slave catchers could turn up anywhere but were less common in central Ohio.

By the late 1840s, all the ferrying and city commerce had inspired talk of yet another way to get across the Ohio River. What if there was a bridge? Engineering and metalwork had advanced to make this feasible, and important bridges were going up in eastern cities. Why couldn't one connect Cincinnati with Covington, Kentucky? It would be an economic boon for both cities, easily paying for itself. The talented engineer John A. Roebling was engaged to design and build the bridge. But illustrating the intractable arguments that slavery led to, Kentuckians balked, seeing the bridge as a potential artery of

Cincinnati's Roebling Bridge under construction; Kentuckians feared that slaves would walk across. *Cincinnati Historical Society.*

The Roebling Bridge became a local landmark and source of pride. *Library of Congress.*

slave getaway. One would think that Kentucky had much to gain in linking to one of the nation's fastest-growing cities; however, in their view, a huge amount of their financial wealth would be able to simply walk across—or be conveyed across—this new bridge. Kentuckians demanded that a clause be placed in the bridge charter holding the construction company liable for this lost economic value. Representatives to the Ohio legislature were displeased and debated the measure at length.[62]

After further delay and maneuverings, work on the bridge finally began in 1856. The Civil War would interfere with construction so that the bridge did not open until 1867. By then, who walked across and who did not no longer mattered. The Roebling Suspension Bridge, a forerunner to Roebling's equally beautiful Brooklyn Bridge, became a treasured landmark of the region. His advanced cabling methods were later used on the Golden Gate Bridge as well.

Chapter 6

HOW THE UNDERGROUND RAILROAD WORKED...AND DIDN'T WORK

The Underground Railroad acquired its new name in the 1830s when it was undergoing a major transformation. As in the old chicken-and-egg riddle, it is debatable what role, if any, the new name played in the movement's expansion. Did the Underground Railroad moniker inspire further growth? Or was it an accurate descriptor of developments that had already occurred? Regardless of the answer, the new name was a case of shrewd branding, even though it would confuse decades of schoolchildren and cause them to wonder where all the locomotives and tunnels were.

Stations, station operators, conductors, depots, freight—these trendy words entered the lexicon of the Underground Railroad, just as they had the shipping world. A noticeable shift was the fact that White people were saying these words to label their own engagement with the movement; it is not unfair to see this as "White people talk." An example was *stockholder*—the word used to describe people who gave money to the effort without directly participating. The Underground Railroad was no longer primarily a "Black people helping Black people" enterprise; dozens—then hundreds—of White people were offering aid as well. Thousands, if you count all the stockholders; hordes were participating through local antislavery societies.

A key change of this period was the addition of the conductor. While there had always been homes, barns and sheds where fugitives were invited to sleep, the conductor service was brand-new. Previously, fleeing slaves were sent on their way with what may or may not have been clear directions and with vague hopes that the destination could be safely reached. Now fugitives

Ohio's network of routes allowed many travel options. *Author's collection.*

were not simply sent on—they were escorted by conductors. This 1830s change was a huge improvement and made the system much safer. There were still occasional slipups and failures, but most freedom seekers who crossed the Ohio River had a high probability of making it to Canada and true freedom. Conductors navigated routes they knew well and were able to run interference in a variety of sticky situations. They knew an alternate itinerary if a suspicious stranger made the original route unwise.

Let's examine how these fugitives and conductors traveled and get right to the matter of tunnels. Something about that word *underground* leads everyone to assume that the Underground Railroad relied on tunnels. However, in all but a tiny handful of cases, that image of the Underground Railroad is wrong. It is no small matter to dig and maintain a tunnel. Only a very few tunnels were used in the Underground Railroad, and some of those had been built for other purposes. Regardless, the belief in tunnels persists.

Take, for example, the town of Springboro in southwest Ohio. Springboro was founded by Quakers and was a well-traveled Underground Railroad site; moreover, it has an extensive tunnel system under its streets. Aha! Generations of later residents believed the tunnels to be connected to the town's Underground Railroad activities, but there is no evidence that these tunnels were used by freedom seekers. The tunnels were part of the infrastructure of the town, carrying water, sewage and so on. But no fugitives.[63]

In a few other locations, there were short tunnels handy for fugitives, but they had been constructed for other reasons. One example was a recommended escape route going under (real) railroad tracks referred to as a tunnel, but it was clearly built by the railroad and is better described as a culvert. Other examples were in the vicinity of rivers. It was not unusual for early riverside homes to have an extra exit from their cellars leading directly down to the waterfront. In some of these, the portion abutting the cellar constituted a short tunnel. A Cincinnati bank had such a construction, used to safely move cash to a docked sternwheeler.[64] There were also a few farmhouses with tunnel-like appendages leading into their cellars. One was a large home in eastern Ohio sitting on a hill above a deep ravine. Because much of the farm's produce was grown in the lower fields, an entrance from that level was dug directly into the home's cellar. It functioned as an extended root cellar and was built for the convenience of the farmer, not the fugitive. Anyone who has ever carried a crate of potatoes or a bushel of apples can see the sense of that.

Regardless of original function, this scattering of tunnels throughout Ohio was likely adapted for fugitive use. In addition, a few station operators may have broken through a cellar wall to add a lower entrance for their fugitive guests; people who excitedly discover these in modern times call them Underground Railroad tunnels, but their short length barely justifies the name.

Existing ravines came in handy, even when they did not lead to tunnels. A scenic section on the north side of Columbus is cut through by a deep ravine—somewhat unusual in relatively flat central Ohio. This formed a private path where fugitives could walk for many yards unseen from nearby homes. But nature put the ravine there—no one dug it. And ravines are not tunnels.

The number of Underground Railroad stations in Ohio with tunnels dug specifically for fugitives is miniscule. The only sure example is excavation under a Cincinnati store owned by noted abolitionist Levi Coffin, where he had fugitives dig through the foundations of adjacent buildings. In this dense urban environment, the length of these tunnels was apparently short; the fugitives burrowing under the city were merely connecting nearby basements.[65] In Circleville, one hundred miles to the east, a longer tunnel fed into the home of Samuel Asbury Moore, another known Underground Railroad participant. But the town of Circleville has a peculiar topographical history that raises serious questions about the Moore tunnel.

The people who established Circleville in 1810 chose to site the new town in the center of a circular mound left by Ohio's ancient Hopewell Indian culture (the design had astronomic significance). They platted a spot for their courthouse in the central roundabout, with two sets of streets surrounding it in concentric circles. One benefit of the unique layout was expected to be the preservation of the ancient earthworks, turning this interesting feature into an asset. But citizens twenty years later disagreed, complaining that travel and lot shapes were just too awkward. They wanted their town to look like other "normal" towns, so in the 1830s, engineers began squaring off the pattern; by 1856, the circles had been replaced by boxes and right angles. In the process, the old earthworks were completely destroyed. Besides erasing this ancient history, the town ruined what would now be regarded as a charming European-style layout, which was later regretted.

The Moore home was one of the town's original buildings, built on its inner circle. Samuel Asbury Moore was born in the house and still lived there during the decades of "squaring off." An ardent abolitionist, he somehow ended up with a lengthy tunnel running from his basement all the way to the edge of town. But who built this tunnel and for what purpose is not clear. As a person of stature in Circleville, perhaps he managed to have it constructed for unseen freedom seekers, or perhaps the town dug it for another infrastructure use, as at Springboro. Could it have anything at all to do with ancient Hopewell ditches adjoining the mounds? The tunnel now barely exists, but decades ago old-timers could recall playing in its end section that opened to a dairy farm. Mostly they remembered being too afraid to crawl very far into the low-ceilinged dark hole. It is now assumed that fugitives traveled through the tunnel, but the notion lacks documentation. No one knows for sure if the old tunnel was actually part of the Underground Railroad.[66]

Beyond the few legitimate Underground Railroad tunnels, false legends abound. There was supposedly a tunnel under the broad Olentangy River near the town of Delaware—a ridiculous notion. Even more bizarre, a West Virginian recently swore to me that a tunnel had been dug under the Ohio River. Residents of Salem, Ohio, boast that several of their grand manors featured tunnels. Similarly, Clevelanders were so insistent that a tunnel had existed under St. John's Episcopal Church, completed in 1838, that they raised money for explorations—twice. The Western Reserve Historical Society two times concluded the church had no tunnels; instead, historians noted that escaping slaves had hidden in the church's belfry and used the bell to warn others if slave catchers were approaching. But no tunnels.[67]

Conveniently, a false saga about tunnels was forming even while the Underground Railroad was active. Residents of Muskingum County once led slave catchers away from their prey by taking them to an old quarry and stating that the fugitives were "down there in those tunnels." This made sense to the gullible men, who eased into the dark and groped along underground. Meanwhile, the fugitive family in question—one that included young children—was guided above ground in broad daylight to a safer location. The ruse of the tunnels helped them safely reach their goal of Canada.[68]

Conversely, there are a few places where tunnels definitely do exist, which believers take as proof of the Underground Railroad. One example of this misguided "back-formation" is at the oldest home in Covington, Kentucky, directly across the river from Cincinnati. The gorgeous 1815 mansion built by Thomas Carneal has a lovely arched brick-lined tunnel leading to its former slave quarters. Carneal has been credited with housing fugitives while they waited to cross the river, but there is zero evidence for this other than the tunnel under his house. In reality, he had it built to spare him the displeasure of watching the comings and goings of the dozens of dark-skinned people required to maintain his palatial home. While it is possible that fugitives received help on the property, it would have been provided by its enslaved workers, certainly not by Carneal, who placed advertisements to recover his missing slaves![69]

Having thankfully finally put the notion of tunnels to rest, let us consider aspects of the Underground Railroad that are indeed true. But with all the misinformation, exaggeration and hazy memories, how do we know what is true? Given the severe penalties for aiding slave escapes and the resulting secrecy, readers might wonder how we have any details at all. The answer is a history professor at The Ohio State University: Dr. Wilbur Henry Siebert.[70]

Wilbur Siebert, born in 1866, grew up in Columbus. After earning his bachelor's degree at Ohio State, he studied at Harvard and in Germany, the birthplace of his father, before returning to his alma mater. Struggling to engage his students, Siebert hit on the idea of assigning them an investigation of the Underground Railroad. He asked for names of any of their relatives or acquaintances who they suspected might have knowledge of the movement. To the names and addresses the class provided, he sent a simple, seven-point query. Letters came back to Dr. Siebert with additional names, prompting

Professor Wilbur Siebert of Ohio State was a key historian of the Underground Railroad. *Ohio History Connection.*

another round of letters—then more. In total, the investigation, which was extended beyond Ohio to the whole United States, yielded thousands of responses. It is the most comprehensive study anywhere of the Underground Railroad.

Today's historians, who operate under higher standards than did Dr. Siebert, sometimes find fault with his methods and his conclusions. But the fact is, had Siebert not done this work, we would know much less about the Underground Railroad. This investigation, first launched in the 1890s, became Siebert's life's work of sixty years' duration. He gleaned details from a generation about to die off; without his inquiries, they would have taken a significant amount of unshared information to their graves.

One of the criticisms of Siebert is particularly valid and must be acknowledged. Because he used his college students as sources for names, he began with an affluent and almost entirely White group of people—he was working in the Jim Crow era, when this did not strike anyone as an obvious problem. Expanding the study to their acquaintances only brought in more prosperous White people. His research design overlooked Black Americans as a source of information and reached no indigenous people at all. Even so, he was able to collect some information on Black station operators and conductors, but not to the degree he could have had he aimed to do so. Later historians have tried to correct for this flaw, with work that commenced a century after the Underground Railroad had ended. After this passage of time, specific names and details of the contributions of the Black population have been difficult to recover.

From the diligent work of Siebert and other historians, what can be concluded in terms of numbers of fugitives helped? No one can be certain, but estimates of the number of fugitive slaves who moved through the Underground Railroad are somewhere between 50,000 and 100,000. To put that in context, the total number of people in bondage at the start of the Civil War was about 4 million. That estimate is taken from a snapshot of a single year, 1860; millions more had lived and died in the six decades or so that the Underground Railroad operated. Even if we allow for a higher overall population count—say 8 million, the numbers suggest that no more about 1 percent of Americans who were ever enslaved escaped by way of the Underground Railroad.[71] (By comparison, about 10 percent of Black Americans relocated during the later Great Migration of the twentieth century—a larger phenomenon that drew from all parts of the South.)

The point that historians make in this analysis is that the Underground Railroad can be overrated. Our modern concept of the Underground Railroad is that it was a far-reaching and prominent opportunity available to all enslaved people; in truth, the Underground Railroad was rather limited. It had specific geographic bounds, the great bulk of which extended north from the Ohio River. But even though the traffic may have been sparse nationally, if you lived on one of its major paths in Ohio, it would have felt like a constant crush of people were headed your way fleeing the bonds of slavery.

A recent attempt to quantify the amount of fugitive traffic through New York City from 1830 to 1860 arrived at the figure of three thousand. A little math applied to activities in the town of Ripley yields that same approximate figure, if not more.[72] All through those decades, the population of New York was more than *three hundred times* Ripley's. Ironically, 3,000 is also cited as the number of fugitives aided by the single individual Levi Coffin operating near the Ohio-Indiana border.[73] These differences in scale should make it clear that the Grand Central Station of this secret kind of railroad was in Ohio, not New York. William Still, active in Philadelphia the last half of this period, is considered by some to be the equivalent of Coffin. In Still's heyday, he knew, or knew of, a large portion of the freedom seekers passing through the City of Brotherly Love—and recorded exactly 649 names. The editor of his memoir claimed that Philadelphia was the most active antislavery city save for Boston, woefully uninformed of the herculean efforts that took place west of the Alleghenies.[74]

Once across the Ohio River, what exactly did fugitives encounter? The typical Underground Railroad station was an ordinary home. If we can now grudgingly accept that they were not all connected by tunnels, surely these homes must have had secret rooms and staircases and such. A few of them did have some special feature, but most did not. They were just houses. Only a small minority of people could afford to build secret compartments into their homes; this was particularly true in the early era of the Underground Railroad dominated by African Americans. Among all races, families were large and offspring usually outnumbered the number of bedrooms. Covert guests slept in any spare space that was available. This included cellars, attics, the floor or barn haylofts. In the rough country of southeastern Ohio, some freedom seekers slept in caves. However, they did not always get dirt floors and second best; one woman recounted that when fugitives arrived at night during her childhood, she would be roused from sleep to make her bedroom available. She remembers drowsily hearing her mother reassure Black guests that they would be safe in the second-floor room. This correspondent of Dr. Siebert declined to say where she spent the rest of the night; perhaps she slid in with her parents.[75]

The only hidden accommodation that most homes could realistically offer was a private section of basement, a space mentioned with some regularity in Siebert's archives. These homes would have been built normally, but with a second wall erected in the basement after the fact. With one end walled off in the same material as the foundation—brick or stone—the main basement looked normal to anyone who was in it. However, it was a bit shorter than it should have been. The only way to enter this partition was through a trapdoor from the first floor, usually cleverly placed in a pantry or closet. Failing that, there were always rag rugs. A number of station operators provided this unique sleeping area, including Udney Hyde in Mechanicsburg. His town home was far from fancy, yet he had thought to add this hidden improvement.

Still, most homes involved in the Underground Railroad were completely ordinary structures with no special adaptations. When it was an African American home, there was little need for stealth. Guests blended into a family and were easily passed off as boarders or visiting cousins. In White-owned homes, freedom seekers found space somewhere. During the day, guests usually kept a low profile, but not always. One White station operator recorded her memory of a strange man approaching her home as she stood working in the kitchen along with a fugitive woman. There was no time to hide, so this resourceful housewife grabbed nearby linens and told her

The typical Underground station was an ordinary home. The Gammons, free Black agents in Springfield, lived here. *Jerry Kenney.*

The home of Udney Hyde in Mechanicsburg. *Ohio History Connection.*

companion to go to the backyard and wash them. Sure enough, the stranger had come to inquire about reported "runaways." The housewife professed lack of knowledge as they casually chatted near the Black woman drawing buckets of water. The presence of a Black washerwoman was so ordinary in the world of the inquirer that he failed to even notice her.

In spite of the ordinariness of most Underground Railroad homes, misperceptions persist. Books have been written on the assumption that all station homes had secret compartments and passageways and that no home could possibly be a part of the Underground Railroad without these elements. The misunderstanding is driven by the fact that a few fine Underground Railroad homes did have concealed spaces, and it is these beautiful homes—built by the well-to-do—that are still standing. More modest Underground Railroad houses were razed long ago or are simply ignored. But now and then you still come across a false wall, a small crawl space hidden behind stairs or a door that leads somewhere unexpected. These imposing houses, now museums or lovingly restored private homes, color present-day views of the Underground Railroad.

Such a home will usually have a second staircase. Back stairs were common in that day of household help and beautiful woodwork, so there is no reason to think they were built with the Underground Railroad in mind. However, alternative egress was indeed useful, though not always as you might expect. On occasional mornings, the daughters of Muskingum County's Guthrie family were told to use the back stairs. This meant that fugitives had arrived during the night were asleep on the floor of the front hall.[76]

How did all these homes, rich and poor, Black and White, connect? Dr. Siebert may have been systematic in his research on the Underground Railroad, but no one was systematic in setting it up. In this sense, the Underground Railroad was nothing like a real railroad: there was no central authority and no one was in charge. This was particularly true in the Ohio Valley, where the Underground Railroad sprang up organically— in a multitude of locations where it made sense geographically. Records in Philadelphia and the East regularly refer to a "Committee" that met and made decisions. In Ohio, with the possible exception of Levi Coffin's work in Cincinnati, there was no semblance of any committee. Each station was independent of the next, although operators collaborated with others nearby.

That meant a lot of collaboration because Ohio had a lot of stations. Every one of the state's eighty-eight counties was somehow touched by the Underground Railroad. In some counties, there might be a route passing by with just a single station; other counties were overlaid with multiple routes and stations. In Highland County, the town of Greenfield alone had literally dozens of stations and conductors; other towns nearby had similar numbers. Stations were located in large cities, towns, small villages or on remote farms. Any size settlement could be made to work, although small villages or rural areas where everyone knew one another were particularly suited for the secret work. Strangers, unusual in these areas, were easily spotted. No matter the community, station operators and conductors were familiar with undercover activity only in their immediate locale; it was best to remain uninformed about stations farther up the lines.

As more and more people participated in the Underground Railroad in the 1840s and 1850s, religious denominations besides Quakers became more noticeable. Presbyterians were very active, a close second to the Quakers, followed by Methodists and Baptists. The latter church was about to splinter over slavery and other nineteenth-century concerns; it is sometimes forgotten that a wing of the Baptist church was staunchly antislavery. The United Brethren Church also took a strong position on the issue. These and other denominations joined the African Methodist Episcopals, who had been doing antislavery work all along.

A final, perhaps surprising, religious group deserves a nod. Our country's Jewish population was scant in the antebellum era; however, there were Jewish businessmen here and there.[77] Some of them, well versed in the flight from slavery, aided escapes. The colorful August Bondi, a Viennese immigrant, first witnessed slavery in New Orleans and could not countenance it; he abruptly left for Kansas to become a pig farmer. There, he interacted with John Brown and helped western Blacks to freedom before enlisting in a Kansas cavalry unit during the Civil War. Bondi also had close ties to Louisville, Kentucky, and possibly assisted antislavery efforts in the Ohio Valley as well.[78] Joseph Friedman had business interests in the river-connected cities of Florence, Alabama and Cincinnati and is remembered for aiding a getaway attempt orchestrated by Philadelphian William Still. Up in Detroit, which sat at the terminus of northwest Ohio's clandestine routes, Rabbi Liebman Adler's congregation of Temple Beth El gave strong support to the Underground Railroad. Congregant Mark Sloman's fur business often took him across the border into Canada; he routinely took freedom seekers along. Many of these fugitives were wearing warm clothes provided

People of many faiths assisted freedom seekers, including a few Jews. *Lee Reynolds, Flickr.*

by temple trustee Emil Heineman, a clothier. Heineman's generosity later extended to the Union army; this immigrant American was said to have outfitted a large number of Michigan troops in fine blue worsted serge.[79]

Clearly the Underground Railroad involved affluent as well as working-class people. The wealthy, such as the furnace owners of Lawrence County, had advantages they learned to use. Quaker businessman Levi Coffin lived part of his life in Cincinnati and part in Indiana, primarily Richmond, just a few miles from the Ohio line. He is called the President of the Underground Railroad, an honorific probably acquired from his openness in antislavery work. Everyone in Richmond knew about Coffin, just as everyone knew about Reverend Rankin in Ripley. Coffin avoided problems by pointedly serving on a Richmond bank board, integral to the commerce of the town—it was not smart to tangle with the bank board. Although Indiana had its share of southern sympathizers, they left Coffin alone.

A freedom seeker's length of stay in any fine or modest home could vary considerably. It might be an hour or less, if someone was feared to be in pursuit, or it could be several weeks. In most cases, speed was not particularly important. Close to the Ohio River, an owner or hired accomplice might be in chase, but farther north this was less common. In central Ohio areas where slave catchers were unlikely, a freedom seeker might purposely dally and rest. With no need for haste, fugitives often remained until the transfer was convenient for the conductor. If there was a reason to "go to town" in three days, why not combine trips? Weather could also be a factor. Many fugitives crossed the Ohio River in the dead of winter, when Lake Erie shipping had shut down until spring. Then there was no reason to rush to the lake, in months when overland travel was difficult anyway. Many accounts left by station operators mention that a certain fugitive had lived with them through the winter. Often it was a whole village or church congregation who took responsibility for all the hosting and providing, especially if a family of freedom seekers was in residence.

When it was time to "transfer freight," station operators or someone of the household could double as a conductor. However, many station operators were happy to host fugitives but less willing to go on the road, with family or farm responsibilities that prohibited travel. In these cases, an acquaintance did the transporting or a conductor could be hired. Well-respected Gist resident John Hudson seems to have made a good chunk of his living transporting freedom seekers. His normal charge was twenty-five cents a journey leg, or not quite twenty dollars per round trip in today's money.

Going could be slow, especially when conductors chose to take less traveled routes that had poorly maintained roads. Regardless of road quality, stations were ideally twelve to fifteen miles apart, so that round trips could be completed in about eight hours, a workable scenario. Trips longer than a single day or night were considered impractical by most conductors.

The extended Vance family of Uniontown, Pennsylvania, and their friends illustrate this need for manageable distance. Opposition to the group's antislavery work in their hometown prompted a half dozen or so households to leave Pennsylvania in the late 1830s. They walked on the new National Road far into Ohio, herding their livestock as they came. There is evidence that they chose to relocate to Highland County because of its heavy Underground traffic and need for additional personnel. In actions that appear deliberate, not happenstance, they even bought farms in specific locations that filled gaps and facilitated travel between the very busy towns of Ripley and Greenfield.[80]

Daytime transfers might be made to look like farm products going to market—and sometimes they were exactly that, at least in part. Anything that made a transfer look like the normal course of affairs was helpful. In nearly all cases, conductors were male, as that was what was expected on the roads. However, some women get credit for conducting; one innovative woman of Ripley assumed the role of a White mother carrying her toddler. She was indeed White, but the child was not. It was "Eliza's" mixed-race grandchild, blanketed and bonneted so that onlookers were none the wiser; the escaping family members were reunited once they had all reached a safe location. Transporting small children required forethought and ingenuity, as the anecdote illustrates. One of the many myths of the Underground Railroad was that even very young children were successfully taught to be silent. Anyone who believes that should probably be wary of unusually attractive real estate offers. Some things are just not true.

Because there is something about a child that adds innocence to any scene, conductors would sometimes take their own sons or daughters along on transfers. The child might even be said to be the reason for the trip: going to Grandma's house or going to town for new shoes—whatever it took. The chances of violence were much less if a child was present. Udney Hyde was probably quite surprised by gunshots when accompanied by his daughter Amanda.

Hyde did not try to keep secrets from his perceptive daughter, but many children were taken on these trips unawares. In the Siebert interviews, conducted about forty years after the Underground Railroad operated, some adults reported that, in hindsight, they suspected that they had been harmlessly used as pawns. One woman described an interesting trip she made with her father hauling cargo to a farm she had never visited. When they arrived, she was taken into the house by a kind lady who fed her gingerbread. From the kitchen, she was unable to see her father's wagon, but he soon returned and said, "All done—time to go." Her memory of the trip, coupled with other facts about her parents she had pieced together, made her realize that her father's wagonload of goods that day had included human beings. As an innocent child enjoying a wagon ride, she had caused no suspicion and had absolutely nothing to reveal.[81]

When a transfer was imminent, a message might be sent to alert the next station operator. This was important if the group was large or included challenges like young children. Depending on the situation, brief notes could be sent by post, by telegram or by a messenger—or not at all. Following is an imagined message: "Expect a good-sized shipment on Tuesday. It will include a freshened cow with her calf born a few months ago plus other young livestock." This meant the next station should be prepared for a family with children, one of which was a baby tended by its mother. Feeding the baby was not going to be an issue, though occasional wailing might be. A recovered authentic message read, "Uncle Tom says that if the roads are not too bad you can look for those fleeces of wool tomorrow. Send them on to test the market and price."[82]

It was not uncommon for operators of Underground Railroad stations to post a signal that it was safe—or unsafe—to approach, messaging meant to be understood by conductors and freedom seekers alike. Even though conductors had become an important element of the Underground Railroad by the mid-1800s, there were still fugitives traveling alone on foot, as Addison White had. Whether this was due to missed connections, a shortage of conductors or a distrust of them is not clear. Lone freedom seekers and escorted groups both needed to recognize which houses were safe to approach. A blanket hanging on a clothesline was the simplest solution. If the blanket was there, it was safe to approach; if it was not, then best to stay away. If you wonder how people kept these messages straight, it seems that people in the neighborhood understood the intended meaning and advised others.

Blankets suggest the matter of quilts, and yes, the displayed bedcovering might have been a quilt. But somehow a notion has gained traction that quilts were sewn with specific symbols that communicated Underground Railroad messages.[83] A book was written on this, but its ideas and bibliography were largely contrived. The whole idea is nonsense. If a person wishes to convey information to others, all under duress, there are more efficient ways of doing it than sitting down and sewing an intricate patchwork quilt! The quilts of that era are imaginative and beautiful, but they were lovingly created for reasons of warmth and aesthetics, not message display. This need not prevent us from admiring heartfelt remembrances of the Underground Railroad in creations stitched by Ohio's prodigious quilt-making talent today.[84]

Another implement thought to have messaging relevance is the ornamental lawn jockey—or groomsman, a type of lawn art once popular throughout the Midwest. It has been proposed that these statues signify a former Underground Railroad station, but the idea is questionable. The theory got a boost from the Piatt family of Logan County headed by Benjamin and Elizabeth Piatt, an interesting and accomplished pair. He was a federal judge who presided over cases in Cincinnati in which he was not known for demonstrating antislavery sentiment. At some point in his career, the Piatts decided to move to the woods of rural Ohio, hours away from his trial work, where they built a very large log house. The Piatts liked big houses; their sons would later build two even more massive ones—something like baronial hunting lodges. In the years those sons were growing up, Judge Piatt was gone a lot, staying in Cincinnati for weeks at a time. Elizabeth Piatt, the story goes, saw slavery much differently from her husband and often hosted fugitives in his absence. Knowing that he was an officer of the government pledged to uphold its laws, she did not wish to put him in the awkward position of breaking the Fugitive Slave Law in his own home. However, she willingly broke it. It is said that she flew a white flag as a signal that it was safe for freedom seekers to approach; grandchildren elaborated that the means of holding this flag was an ornamental lawn jockey.[85]

There are problems with this tale. It is not clear that lawn jockeys were even manufactured before the late nineteenth century, when the information was shared. Some have thought to wonder if the kids concocted more than just the statue's supporting role. Did Siebert's correspondent engage in a bit of embellishment, or was all of this made up?[86] Most of Siebert's findings can be corroborated in multiple sources, but it happens that this story cannot. If it is an entire prevarication, we lose an intriguing story of a wife's duplicity within a marriage. However, reports of her antislavery work may well be accurate, with the detail of a lawn jockey its only falsehood. No matter what did and didn't go on at the Piatts' big log home, the imagination of its descendants may be the origin of the lawn jockey legend.

Lawn jockeys or no, what was life like for freedom seekers on the move? In the earliest years of the Underground Railroad, travel was mostly by foot, and movement was at night. Fugitives conducted by the Rankins kept to this pattern, with a Rankin son (who would be returning home that same night) riding horseback while freedom seekers walked in the shadows along the side of the road. As time went on, wagons became more prevalent and travel often occurred in daytime. A canvas back on the wagon might suffice to keep fugitives hidden, but even more secure was a false bottom. These wagons were jerry-rigged with an added floor allowing about eighteen inches of space beneath. Wagon uses could be more inventive than that, however. Levi Coffin once staged a fake funeral to convey a large group in broad daylight. A hearse followed by a closed carriage, with curtains thoughtfully drawn for "mourners," efficiently did the trick.[87]

If fugitives were transported under a load of hay, it did not much matter what they wore. But this was not the only strategy. Fugitives sometimes wore high-quality clothing—either taken from their owners or later supplied. Well-dressed and confident in demeanor, they just moved about in the manner of free people. One adult who responded to Dr. Siebert said that visitors to her home had greatly confused her during her childhood because they wore fancy suits and nice silk dresses. Her mother, who could not afford such a dress, did everything she could to feed and help these people and give them even more items. These remembrances, and an understanding of the station her parents ran, only made sense to her many years later.[88]

Hiding in plain sight was a more common aspect of the Underground Railroad than people now realize, and it allowed more comfortable modes of travel. After 1830, Ohio's canals were crucial to freedom seekers. A towpath for mules and muleskinners paralleled each canal; since boats ran only in daytime, these paths were deserted after hours. Both of Ohio's main canals ran in north–south directions; their towpaths provided fine northerly nocturnal routes. During the day, canals were busy places of commerce, with wagons coming and going; certainly some wagon sides concealed more than farm goods. There was much unloading and loading at warehouses in places like Dayton and Roscoe Village, providing options for subterfuge. Roscoe, named for an English abolitionist, was adjacent to Coshocton; African American Prior Foster had been helping fugitives through the town even before its canal was completed.[89] Now many men worked loading boats and had opportunities to hide themselves or companions among the cargo. This would have been with the full knowledge of the boat captain, as canalboats were not large. Canal docks constituted important Underground Railroad depots connecting land

Ohio's main canals ran north–south and were part of its Underground Railroad. *Library of Congress.*

and water travel; the map of Ohio's covert routes shows a strong convergence with its canals.

Except for towpaths, anything said about canalboats can also be said of trains, which came into play about 1840. Canalboats and trains both offered the best option of all: paid, ticketed travel. Yes, Underground Railroad fugitives moved on real railroads. Openly doing so required that travelers sport expensive-looking clothing; scores of people riding on trains looking like affluent free Blacks were actually freedom seekers. In the large swaths of Ohio with antislavery leanings, some onlookers may have suspected the truth but chose not to interfere.

The women of many cities and towns formed antislavery sewing circles to produce the necessary attire. Merchants and shoemakers gave goods; other items were funded by donations. Fundraising also paid for canal and railway tickets, although some fugitives worked for wages to buy their own. Nearly every Ohio county had an antislavery society; the United States being a capitalist-minded country, clever financial schemes developed. For example, it seems that travelers approaching Cleveland had to purchase tickets to its downtown terminus even when they planned to disembark at a suburban station. This resulted in a lot of leftover tickets with small amounts of value remaining, like a pile of partially used metro cards today. An antislavery group in Alliance collected these and worked out a deal with the rail line for an equivalent amount of new tickets.[90] In addition, rail conductors in the Cleveland area were friendly to fugitive passengers, directing engineers to approach stations slowly so that any rider who wanted to exit short of the crowded platform could do so.

Some fugitives who got new clothes switched to the opposite gender. If slave catchers had received a specific description to look for, portraying the opposite gender was a smart move for someone with the body type to carry it off. Both men and women did this. The elaborate bonnets women wore in that era were a benefit to deception, as was Quaker clothing. Some disguised fugitives altered their skin tone. Light-skinned freedom seekers used burnt cork to darken themselves; others used powder or flour to lighten.

Freedom seekers rode trains as ticketed passengers or hidden among cargo. *Smithsonian Institution*.

Above: The Little Miami was one of Ohio's earliest and most successful railroads, linking Cincinnati to Cleveland via transfer. *Ohio History Connection.*

Opposite: Quaker Phebe Benedict of Alum Creek. The work of feeding and clothing fugitives was done by women. *Ohio History Connection.*

Undoubtedly, the greatest achievement in costuming, not to mention acting, was performed by Ellen Craft in the East. For days, the light-skinned Ellen portrayed a sickly young man traveling north for medical help via boat and train, with her actual husband serving as her slave. Alleged poor eyesight and a broken arm concealed the fact she could neither read nor write. The Crafts later learned to do both and documented this masquerade in their memoir. Similar theatrics may have occurred on Ohio trains, although they probably paled next to the extreme measures of the Crafts, who were traveling through the South.[91]

Trains were the site of several fraught escapades in Ohio, including the rescue of a John Price, who fled from Maysville, Kentucky; known as the Oberlin-Wellington rescue, the events are fully described in other sources. Fugitives were snatched off trains by slave catchers and by antislavery adherents alike. In 1841, about the same time train travel commenced, an Ohio judge gave the antislavery crowd a helpful opening; he declared that Ohio law did not recognize the institution of slavery, so that slaves were legally free within the bounds of the state even when accompanied by an

owner.[92] Temporary freedom could also occur if an enslaved traveler briefly disembarked from a riverboat in Cincinnati or like port. On early railroads, route changes due to problems on the tracks caused some surprised people to find themselves in a station where slaves were technically free. The enslaved did not always realize this, but abolitionists did.

Men attending an antislavery meeting the summer of 1854 in Salem were notified that an approaching train held a young slave girl traveling with a couple who claimed ownership. Upon its arrival, the men boarded the train, grabbed the terrified girl and removed her. They had no legal documents but were not challenged. Money was collected for the girl's support, and a local family raised her as one of their own. They named her Abby Kelly Salem for a well-known abolitionist speaker and the site of her liberation. If any of these people had concerns for the status of the girl's biological family and her separation from them, these were not recorded.[93]

Another novel way fugitives moved on trains was in boxes. After Henry "Box" Brown gained fame for having himself crated and shipped to Philadelphia, several tried the same tactic into Ohio, with mixed success.[94] The tactic required both determination and slight stature.

Near the midpoint of the nineteenth century, and particularly in response to the 1850 Fugitive Slave Law, transporting fugitives grew less secretive. Many conductors now traveled openly in daylight. These overt operations were more likely in some parts of the state than in others. A varied settlement pattern in early Ohio affected travel choices; writer Colin Woodard has identified three unique "cultures" cutting across the state. Ohio's southerly population group is Appalachian. New Englanders may have established some of the first riverside towns there, but the area was soon engulfed by people relocating from Virginia, Kentucky or Tennessee. Typically Scots-Irish, these people were treated poorly in Europe and took whatever hilly land was left to get out of the old country. In Woodard's analysis, this group is distrustful of government but quick to fight to protect their own, seeing honor in fighting for clan. The middle of Ohio is characterized by "Midlanders" out of Pennsylvania, a mix of English Quakers, Germans and others, accustomed to existing with a live-and-let-live attitude within a mixed society. Most value personal endeavor and prosperity over politics. The "Yankees" who settled Northeast Ohio, coming across the Erie Canal as well as land routes, have a greater tendency to take ideological positions. They first settled this country in organized towns and prefer a fully formed government, which has treated them well in the past. Strictures, mandates and firmly held beliefs are a part of their world.[95]

Ohio's attitude toward slavery varied within the state due to population differences. *"The American Nations Today" by Sean Wilkinson; from* AMERICAN NATIONS: A HISTORY OF THE ELEVEN RIVAL REGIONAL CULTURES OF NORTH AMERICA *by Colin Woodard, copyright © 2011 by Colin Woodard. Used by permission of Viking Books, an imprint of Penguin Publishing Group, a division of Penguin Random House LLC. All rights reserved.*

Freedom seekers would have noticed changes as they moved through these three stripes of society. Outside of safe stations, they were treated as unwelcome outsiders in southern Ohio. But farther north, fugitives encountered a population that regarded them more neutrally. One example is a meal Addison White received at a central Ohio home. Seeing his hunger, the homeowner brought him a well-mounded plate but asked that Addison move on immediately after eating and tell no one he had been there. In typical Midlander behavior, this farmer was willing to help a fellow human being but wanted no further involvement in controversy. Closer to Lake Erie, freedom seekers were among people who had specifically chosen their side of a difficult argument. In some northern towns, fugitives could walk openly down the street in no danger of confrontation. It was the slave catchers who were the unwelcome outsiders here.

Ashtabula Harbor in the 1800s. Many fugitives left for Canada from Toledo, Sandusky, Cleveland or here. *Ohio History Connection.*

This antislavery attitude extended to Lake Erie ports, the final departure point for many freedom seekers. Captains were open to taking on fugitives; perhaps some collected fares for this, although records suggest that many provided the service gratis.[96] This differed markedly from life on the Mississippi and Ohio Rivers, which were oriented to southern commerce. Knowingly transporting fugitives was a risky (and rare) act for captains of the riverboats, who stood to lose business if found out. But boats plying the lake to Ontario were less burdened by slave-owning customers and followed a different conscience.

"Yankee" northern Ohio includes Cleveland, Oberlin and Hudson, the childhood home of John Brown—he later spent a decade in Akron in this same locale. In a side note, Ulysses S. Grant's father, Jesse, lived with the Brown family in Hudson during his apprenticeship in their tannery business. It is one of many towns in this part of Ohio with central greens amid a precise layout punctuated by church spires. There was organization to the pattern because the town fathers planned it that way. In the hills of the southern part of state, each building was where some individual decided to build it. Only the streets imposed order on what would have otherwise been a higgledy-piggledy pattern.

Many of the tense clashes of Ohio's Underground Railroad took place near its southern edge. A rough crowd lived in these hardscrabble

Polly Jackson fought slave catchers with boiling water and a butcher knife. *Ohio History Connection.*

hills, where slave catchers regularly roamed. Physical defense was often a necessity. The free Black woman Polly Jackson of Brown County was known to throw boiling water on slave catchers or fight them off with a butcher knife. To the east in Gallia County, another woman may have done her one better. In this incident, men and women armed with loaded guns were guarding a house while fugitives hid in its root cellar. The women had started pots of water to boil. A neighbor identified as Mrs. Griffin brusquely arrived and reminded them, "Don't forget to throw in the cornmeal! Gruel sticks better and it burns."[97]

The town of Salem, founded by Quakers, exists near the border of Yankee and Midlander world and has elements of both. Two locals, the Coppoc brothers, rode with John Brown all the way to Harpers Ferry. Barclay Coppoc escaped after the failed mission, but Edwin was hanged, as was Brown. When Edwin's body was retrieved and brought back to Salem for burial, two thousand residents of the small town attended his service as well as a picnic afterward.[98] Salem, home of an important abolitionist newspaper, the *Antislavery Bugle*, had long been known as a haven for freedom seekers. Slave catchers were said to be afraid to go to Salem. It seems that one of their own was badly beaten there and barely lived to tell about it. It is not known who did the pummeling, but Quakers were not passive milquetoasts. They had a steely resolve—perhaps a few had steely fists as well.

Woodard's delineations of settlement across Ohio are useful, but they do not explain everything. The geography of the Underground Railroad can be confusing. For example, both Dayton and Zanesville were founded by Virginians and are said to have been proslavery towns that fugitives avoided. Yet both had extremely important Underground Railroad stations. Deeper investigation reveals that these stations were outside the town limits of that era. Today's Oakwood, a leafy neighborhood of fine old homes and one of Dayton's earliest suburbs, was then farmland; along with Carillon Park, this span bordering the Miami and Erie Canal was once a hotbed of undercover action. Similarly, across the Muskingum River from Zanesville was the village of Putnam, named for Ohio founder and antislavery thinker David Putnam. Harriet Beecher Stowe's brother Reverend William Beecher, an abolitionist Presbyterian minister, led vital Underground activity there just beyond the eyes and ears of a proslavery crowd. Putnam was long ago absorbed into the larger town of Zanesville, which is very proud of the historic neighborhood today.

Chapter 7

JOHN PARKER OF RIP-ROARING RIPLEY

John Parker was the smartest person in the room. It did not matter what room he was in—he was always the smartest. It could be in his foundry working with employees; it could be in a room of Ripley antislavery colleagues convening to discuss a knotty problem. Or it could be in a slave pen—John Parker had been in those too. In his youth, John Parker had been enslaved.[99]

Born in 1827 in Virginia, Parker believed himself to be the son of an important plantation owner there, but he could not be sure where "there" was. He had been sold away from mother and home at such a young age that he never knew the name of his town, his plantation, his owner or maybe not even that of his mother. He was pulled from all that at the age of eight and made to walk to Richmond to a slave sale. A kindly older enslaved man tried to comfort him during those awful days, but it was no substitute for a mother's care. What Parker mainly remembered was anger.

His next journey was one of many weeks from Richmond to Mobile, Alabama; Parker distracted himself by smashing flowers and trying to kill birds on the way. In Mobile, he was purchased by a physician.[100] Parker was still young, and his duties seem to have been light. He drove the doctor to his house calls, but there was plenty of free time for carousing with the doctor's two sons, who were about his own age. They roamed fields doing whatever boys do. He taught them the hunting and fishing tricks he knew; back at home, they taught him to read. Little John must have been something of a novelty, picking up reading at breakneck pace. He was soon devouring books from the shelves of the home's large library. The doctor seemed to be aware of his literary proficiency but did not mind.

Parker's education almost continued at Yale, in vicarious fashion, when it was decided that he would accompany his White companions to college as a servant. But while they were all en route to New Haven, interaction with a Quaker abolitionist made the good doctor think better of it, and he had John return to Mobile. The scholars might have done better with Parker's assistance; it is not clear that they passed the Yale entrance exams and ever attended classes.

Back in Mobile in a newly quiet house, the doctor faced the problem of what to do with his young slave. Life as a houseboy was not going to suit Parker, who presumably lacked a gentle, obsequious nature. What he had instead was a keen mind, an engineer's knack and a hot temper. The doctor, always kind, seems to have understood him. He decided that Parker should be apprenticed in the trades, but a brief experience with a plasterer did not work out. Parker was mistreated and got embroiled in a scuffle, after which he had to run away to save himself. Thus began an extended wild adventure of hideaways, capture and escape that repeated itself at least four times. Parker was on his own in the Deep South trying to reach some form of safety and freedom, but there was little opportunity for it. He knew that the Mississippi River could take him north to freedom, but a journey of that duration required food and water; without someone providing sustenance, it was impossible. He hid in several boats, but even if he was not discovered, hunger and thirst eventually forced him out of his spot in a cargo hold and he was caught yet again. If he managed to escape one bad situation, he hopped another boat and inevitably got into another. The result was that he looped back and forth between Mobile and New Orleans and partway up the Mississippi, although he does not seem to have gotten much farther than Vicksburg. Secluded in a dark hold, he rarely knew where he was. His final capture led to ten months in a New Orleans jail, but by using his sharp wits he was able to escape even that. All this cat-and-mouse activity consumed the better part of a year. The final indignity occurred after he boarded a boat in New Orleans for his getaway without taking note of its destination. Realizing that it was bound not for the north but for Mobile, his starting place, he sat pondering what to do. A hand suddenly gripped his shoulder; it was the doctor, who had ironically booked passage on this same boat. With his usual aplomb and now cognizant of the plasterer's drunken rages, the doctor quipped, "Well, there you are," and their congenial relationship simply started up again.

This time, Parker was apprenticed to a foundry, a better experience. The eighteen-year-old learned everything rapidly and excelled in ironwork. However, his problems fitting in continued, especially with supervisors who had a weak grasp of their trade. Parker often knew more than they and had little interest in hiding it. This was in the days before assembly lines and shared projects; each worker in a foundry individually turned out his widgets and gadgets. Parker outpaced everyone in quality and quantity. His output annoyed others; also annoying were the fine, proud clothes that he bought with the extra money he earned. He even stood up for himself against random criticism and small slights, shocking behavior from a slave.

The predictable happened. More trouble occurred at the foundry, and the doctor had finally had enough. He informed Parker that he had decided to sell him off as a field hand in a sale three days hence. Now here was a true difficulty and certain death sentence; however, Parker devised yet another getaway. He decided to approach a woman who was one of the doctor's patients. He had been in Mrs. Ryder's home several times and liked her. Parker proposed that she buy him for $1,800, which he understood to be his value; he could pay her back plus interest with his extra earnings from the foundry. She was at first resistant, but he seems to have been a good salesman in addition to everything else. At the last minute, she agreed, and he went to live with her. Newly motivated, Parker was able to increase both his production and his self-control at the foundry. He did this even as his first invention was stolen from him. The foundry had been filling orders for a certain part; Parker saw how to make an improved version and showed his supervisor. Soon the idea and all the added proceeds were credited to the supervisor, but Parker held his tongue. Despite impediments like this, Parker churned out his stellar production and paid off Mrs. Ryder, now also his friend, just as he had proposed. He was finally free. She hoped that he would stay at her Mobile home; he had liked living there, even though it lacked a fine library like the doctor's. But Mrs. Ryder was unaware of his angry parting words with that old supervisor; besides, he had heard about a foundry in Indiana. It was best to go north.

Parker would not have learned this in Alabama, but Indiana was relatively unwelcoming to Black residents; he stayed in the Hoosier State only briefly, after hearing of opportunities in Cincinnati. Beginning in 1845, he spent four years becoming familiar with the workings of the Queen City and its Underground Railroad. He initially stayed on the sidelines of the latter but before long he was approached about crossing the river to help two teen girls flee. They were fifty miles upriver across from Ripley, a town he had never heard of. Enjoying his freedom and his Cincinnati life, he had no interest in the mission—going into slave territory was the last thing he needed. Even some White abolitionists caught there did not return with their lives—the fate of a "mulatto" man aiding runaways would be even gorier.

After being asked several times and told the girls' dire story, he finally agreed. This first foray across the river was successful, but not without slipups. He met the girls at the appointed time and place but was startled to see that both were fat. Then he realized that each girl was wearing every fancy dress she could get her hands on, one over the other, four apiece on each girl. Parker also realized that he had not adequately thought through his return strategy; he had great difficulty finding a boat and a set of oars. At length, the threesome were finally settled in a boat, the teens nearly hidden under a heap of hoopskirts. The fancy hats they were wearing turned out to be blessing; the boat was very leaky, and Parker set them to work bailing with their silk bonnets.

After this shaky start, Parker's skill as a furtive conductor improved. He, with his new wife, the former Miranda Boulden, decided to move upriver to Ripley. Their family grew as he established his own foundry business there. But he kept going across the river at night; he returned multiple times and was soon guiding large groups into Ohio.

Parker was well aware that life on the two sides of the river was lived differently. According to one historian, "Travelers on the Ohio River…often noticed the disparity between the economic development on the opposite banks of the river. On the north shore, the river towns of Ohio and Indiana bustled and throbbed, and the farms between the towns thrived. On the south bank, Virginia and Kentucky comparatively slumbered, with few towns and mile after mile of apparent wilderness."[101]

Ripley may have been unlike Maysville, but it had not been so different from Cincinnati in the early years. River trade caused the two Ohio towns to mutually boom and stretch at the seams. Both packed hundreds of barrels of pork to send south; high profits convinced residents to tolerate squealing, stinking zones not far from their respectable neighborhoods. In cotton-growing areas, so much money was made from the fiber that planters had no interest in growing the usual food products—they could be ordered from up north. Farmers, coopers, weavers, salt-makers, millers and packers all worked to keep up as innumerable barrels and bags of pork, lard, cornmeal and flour were shipped downriver. Cincinnati was Ohio's biggest shipper of these products, but Ripley was in second place not far behind.[102]

John Parker found opportunity in Ripley, but by the year of his relocation, the Queen City's advantages were causing it to outpace and supplant the smaller towns. Cincinnati had the Miami River, the basis of the Miami and Erie Canal. It was closer to the action of southern trade, just past the Indiana state line. Also, if a Black person, enslaved or free, managed to go upriver, Cincinnati was where they likely went ashore. In the first half of the nineteenth century, nearly three-fourths of Ohio's Black population resided in Cincinnati, the largest gathering of free Blacks in the entire old Northwest Territory.[103]

It is widely acknowledged—then and now—that the single busiest Underground Railroad depot in the nation was Cincinnati. A lot of good happened there, mixed with a lot of bad. The good centered on people in the Black community like Peter Clark, David Nickens, Peter and Sarah Fossett, Frances Scroggins-Brown and John Malvin. They were joined by White activists like Anna Donaldson, abolitionist printer James Birney, Lane Theological Seminary professor Theodore Weld and civil rights lawyers John Joliffe, Salmon P. Chase and Rutherford B. Hayes. Almost in a class of his own was Levi Coffin, the so-called President of the Underground Railroad.[104] Coffin, a prosperous businessman, reveled in that title. One of his businesses was a "fair trade" store that sold only products made by free people; the merchandise was not all easy to locate and acquire. Slavery-related occurrences in Cincinnati could fill whole volumes—and have. Birney's press was trashed, Whites rioted against Blacks, major court cases were tried and tense mobs milled around courthouses and jails. Coffin figured prominently throughout much of it. A full accounting of events and individuals is too voluminous to name.

But Ripley had its own advantages. Per capita, it was far busier than Cincinnati in fugitive traffic. Underground Railroad station keepers and conductors generally had an easier time operating in towns rather than in big cities with a lot of unknown people walking about. Ripley served well in size and geography, sitting on a narrow bend of the river. The Natchez Trace, the main north–south road of the South, ended across the river in Maysville; from there, a short downstream float delivered travelers to Ripley. High bluffs rise visibly behind Ripley, drained by two creeks that approximate a straight north direction, useful for navigation or for covering one's path if trackers were in chase. The wooded hills ahead offered cover and were dotted with friendly settlements. In short, if you were sent to scout out the whole Ohio Valley for a spot to locate an effective Underground Railroad station, you could hardly do better than Ripley, Ohio.

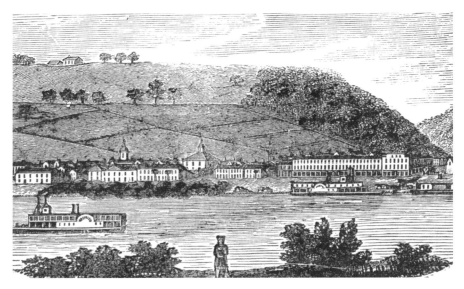

Ripley prospered from river commerce in the 1800s. John Rankin's hilltop home is visible in this 1847 woodcut. *Ohio History Connection.*

Ripley's greater strength was the bevy of antislavery people who had been gathering in the area for as long as Ohio had been a state. Brown County was a key entry point into the state's Virginia Military District, positioned at the midpoint of its Ohio River border, and many southerners came. But in a slight twist of stereotype, many of the Virginians who came to Ohio were those willing to forego slavery. In fact, some celebrated leaving it. Ripley founder James Poage, a longtime military veteran and wilderness surveyor, arrived from Virginia in 1804 with a literal boatload of slaves and promptly freed them. It wasn't just slavery they demolished; after coming ashore, the group immediately tore apart their flatboats to build cabins with the wood. This was their town. The next year, Dr. Alexander Campbell, a Virginian by birth who had studied medicine in Lexington, moved to adjoining Adams County, escorting his freed slaves. He became known as Ohio's first abolitionist, serving in the Ohio legislature and then the U.S. Senate. He is remembered for calmly mounting his horse and riding back to Ohio when the British torched Washington during the War of 1812. He quit politics; the next year, he moved his family to Ripley and became its first physician. By then, Presbyterian minister James Gilliland had been preaching for ten years in Red Oak, a village just to the north. Also early to the abolitionist label, he had declared this dogma from his pulpit in South Carolina and was effectively driven north.

Ripley's first mayor was Nathaniel Collins, a carpenter; sometime around 1815, he began occasionally hiding fugitives in the cornfield behind his house or in the coffins he made in his shop—no slave catcher ever ventured a peek inside the latter. His wife, Nancy, the daughter of a Presbyterian minister back east, was a partner in deception. His sons were similarly active in antislavery work, as were the sons of some other families of the town. The Beasley brothers, both physicians, settled in Ripley at some point. Thomas McCague became wildly wealthy after relocating from Kentucky with his wife, Catherine (Kitty). Some said that he had the largest flour mill and pork-packing operation on the Ohio River. His revenues were parlayed into banking; he floated a large loan to desperate New York financiers during the Panic of 1837. Both Thomas and Kitty were Underground Railroad operatives, although he liked to keep a low profile because much of his business was with the South. Kitty was fearless; she is the woman who rode through town, pretending the blanketed Black baby she held on her lap was her own.

Most of these individuals were people of the South fighting a scourge they well knew. They frequently collaborated with the free Blacks living at the town's outskirts on Africa Hill or at Gist. This brave group included Rhoda Jones, Billy Marshall, Moses Cumberland, Polly Jackson and the literate siblings Sally and John Hudson.

We are just getting to the revered leader of the Ripley team, Reverend John Rankin, another Presbyterian minister, who arrived in 1822 with his wife, Jean, and their young family. The couple were both Tennessee born. They first moved into a house in town near his church, but bothered by some of the rowdies around—not all in Ripley were of the antislavery sort—he decided to build a house on a high hill at the edge of town. While still on Front Street, he got word that his brother in Virginia had purchased slaves. Horrified, Reverend Rankin wrote his brother a series of letters that were published in 1825 as *Letters on Slavery*. The copies initially languished in a warehouse, with Rankin lacking the funds to market them. But in the 1830s, his prospects improved. The Rankins were cozily settled in the new hilltop home, and a major publisher rereleased the title. The book became a hit, widely read in the North; excerpts ran in abolitionist newspapers such as *The Liberator*. Rankin embarked on a series of speaking tours and was often absent from Ripley. But no matter—his six sons conducted Underground Railroad transports, while Jean and their four daughters managed food and clothing supplies.

Rankin was never a prosperous man. His large family barely fit into the squat brick home, but when freedom seekers came, space was found

The Rankin family. Adam Lowry Rankin is absent, and one daughter is deceased. Philanthropist Arthur Tappan is at far right. *Ohio History Connection*.

The Rankin home today. *Walter Havighurst Special Collections, Miami University*.

somewhere. However, it was preferable that fugitives be briskly escorted on to the quiet village of Red Oak. Besides limited beds, the greater concern was the renown of the Rankin house. Everyone on both sides of the river knew that it harbored runaways; Reverend Rankin thundered as much from his pulpit. Fugitives could not rest easy for long in the Rankin house or barn—best that one of his plucky sons saddle up and move them on.

Reverend Rankin may have bookishly focused on speaking and organizing, but his boys could be tough. Once, the group, Jean included, successfully defended their home in what amounted to a pitched gun battle. The importance of the whole Rankin family cannot be overstated. Easterners highly celebrated for their antislavery work said that it was Ohio's John Rankin who inspired them. One devotee was *Liberator* publisher William Lloyd Garrison of Boston. Another was Harriet Beecher Stowe's brother Henry Ward Beecher, who went so far as to reassign some of Lincoln's credit for emancipation. When asked who abolished slavery, he is said to have responded, "Rev. John Rankin and his sons did it."[105]

Through his many contacts, Rankin linked Ripley to the outside world. For a time, he operated an academy; one of his students was Hiram Grant from Georgetown, an easy ride and one Underground Railroad stop away. The antislavery Grant family had been familiar with that quiet traffic for years; their first home in Point Pleasant had been right on the Ohio River, with a feeder stream running along their property through a deep creek bed. It is likely that some freedom seekers did so as well; more trails bracketed the tiny village at Moscow on one side and New Richmond on the other. Hiram was not overly bookish, but he studied enough to avoid work in the family tannery, a smelly, disgusting business he hated. A West Point appointment extended this reprieve. At the military academy, a mistake was made on his registration papers; the young man amiably learned to answer to this new name, Ulysses S. Grant.[106]

The Rankin family intermingled with faculty and students of Cincinnati's Lane Theological Seminary, briefly a center of abolitionist thought in the West. Around 1830, the struggling seminary was identified by the wealthy Tappan family of New York as a place where antislavery thought might flourish. They funded and expanded the small school, recruiting the important eastern minister Lyman Beecher to be its president. Among the family members who came to Ohio was his twenty-one-year-old daughter, Harriet. The well-educated Harriet took part in seminary events and found that she was attracted to Professor Calvin Stowe; the two married in early 1836—after a lot of other drama had ensued.

Ulysses S. Grant, born and raised nearby, had links to Ripley. *Library of Congress.*

In 1834, Lane had held a series of debates and speeches on the subject of slavery; the abolitionist points put forth were considered highly radical at the time. Much of this action was student-driven; the students also began programs of working, studying and worshiping directly with Cincinnati's large Black population. Conservatives of the city became alarmed; in the end, a mob threatened to shut down the slavery debates—indeed, the whole school. Trustees at Lane realized that things had gotten out of hand; claiming safety concerns, they voted to disallow all antislavery activities. A little to the north, Miami University had already passed a similar measure. Returning from summer break in fall 1834, the core group of fervent Lane students arrived eager to resume activities only to find that their extracurricular interests had been suspended. There was to be no discussion on the matter.

A majority of the students responded by leaving the school. About fifty in number, they initially went across town and established another seminary with the intent of continuing their work in the Black community. But a chance contact with an Oberlin official changed their course. Oberlin College, brand new and far to the north, was willing to work with the seminarians and reassured them their interests would be tolerated—even welcomed—at the school. This was no doubt sincere, but Oberlin administrators could not fail to notice that Tappan money would arrive with the group. The ex-Lane contingent, which included students of both White and Black races and selected faculty members, arrived at Oberlin in the fall of 1835. Liberalism at Oberlin was thereby cemented, forged by the "Lane Rebels" out of the racial tinderbox of Cincinnati.

But not everyone went north. Among those who stayed at Lane were the Beechers and Professor Stowe. Reverend Rankin had attended the slavery debates, mixing with Lane leadership and becoming well acquainted with this friendly threesome. Lyman Beecher and Harriet even stayed in the Rankin home on a visit to Ripley. One of Rankin's sons, Adam Lowry Rankin, would attend Lane in 1836 and become close with Professor Stowe, by then Harriet's husband. Over time, this Cincinnati group heard many of Ripley's anecdotes, including the "Underground Road" taken by Tice Davids and the mother teetering across an ice floe. This exchange of information is a large part of what led to Harriet's famous book and the supposed remark by Lincoln when he later met her: "So you're the little lady who started our great war!"

When Parker arrived in Ripley in 1849, these events, minus Lincoln's comment, were all in the past. He was the latecomer to Ripley's formidable group of antislavery activists. Parker had known Levi Coffin and others in Cincinnati; he believed that this new group was far superior to the collection of individual egos in the larger town. What he found in Ripley was a dedicated, smoothly operating team that mixed easily with one another, regardless of income, education, race or religiosity. Parker seamlessly fit right in. When you have the smartest man in the room, next to the richest, the most fervent (Rankin), as well as the mayor, the town doctors, a newspaper editor and the help of wives and various family members, there is little you cannot do. And Ripley did.

Due to its brisk river business, Ripley's population had doubled in the decade prior to Parker's arrival, but at 1,800, it was still a fraction of Cincinnati's. In an interview during his elder years, Parker claimed that 300 of those 1,800 residents were members of Ripley's Antislavery Society. Perhaps the more revealing metric is the six shoemakers who had busy shops in town.[107] In an era when even the wealthy had just a few pairs of footwear and children's shoes were passed down within a family, how exactly were six shoemakers staying busy? Fugitives. Most enslaved people wore cheap shoes, and unless they had absconded with owners' shoes that fit them, their footwear was almost always in terrible shape. If a journey had been long, maybe ropes or straps held soles and uppers together, sandal-like. Not only would bad shoes give out on the further journey ahead, their "slave shoes" would certainly give them away. So, shoemakers and cobblers labored long, paid by the antislavery societies.

Parker assisted with the normal Underground Railroad activities in town. Like everyone else, he burned his relevant records when the Fugitive Slave Law was passed, and his estimate of the numbers of fugitives he helped varied with each telling.[108] Five hundred is a fair guess. By contrast, the large Rankin family, in Ripley two decades longer than Parker, assisted around two thousand.[109] That output was from just two households of a large team. There was much collaboration among all; Tom Collins, Nathaniel's son, was Parker's go-to undercover colleague. But unlike the rest, only Parker would venture into Kentucky for fugitive-fetching missions.

John Parker was accustomed to being the smartest person around, and he was not above some intellectual snobbery. He did not think highly of the slaves he brought out of Kentucky, calling them riffraff. A lack of mental acuity was the very reason these people needed his help, in his view. If they were smarter, they could have figured it out themselves. When he was guiding a large group one still night, they repeatedly broke out in loud arguments, and it was only by threatening them at gunpoint that he got them to quiet down. This, in fact, was the key reason conductors armed themselves; guns were used to enforce instant compliance of freedom seekers more than they were used against slave catchers. Another time, he arrived to guide a mixed-gender group to find that one of the women had tied all her pots and pans to her bundle. Puttering about her cabin making preparations to leave, she was already clanging of tin and iron. Parker often made his fugitives leave their bulky packs behind, this one for sure.

Parker respected those who traversed these lands unaided, and he was genuinely impressed by freedom seekers who came from southern Kentucky or Tennessee. Those trips took great care and planning, and Parker considered the fugitives who undertook them to be his intellectual equals. New arrivals from a distance always explained that they had prepared while patiently waiting for the corn to ripen so they would have something to eat on the way. Cornfields paved the way out of the upper South. If cotton could grow there, leaving would have been much harder.

Parker was able to move with relative ease through the woods of northern Kentucky, which he called the "borderland," although he noted that additional clearings and farms complicated his travels over time. This was not the fine land of the Bluegrass farther south; newcomers here were settling for forest—second best in the state. The area was patrolled each night, but Parker enjoyed outsmarting this White strain of riffraff too. He had a few close calls but defended himself ably with fists and a knife. During one of his Kentucky incursions, he was stunned to learn that there was a $1,000 price on his head, a huge amount in those days. This was not hearsay: he saw the sign himself. Seasoned in stealth, he completed the mission, but the dead-or-alive reward was disconcerting. The bounty changed his life for a time—even on the Ohio side, where he had to wield his knife against one attacker. During another attempt on his life, he was aided by his wife, a White employee and even his faithful dog. But, as usual, Parker, a veritable genius, was smarter than those trying to kill him; after the third failed attempt, the Kentuckians seemed to lose interest.

Of all Parker's Underground work north and south of the Ohio River, an incident involving an infant was the most daring. It seems that a young, enslaved couple living near the river wanted to run, but their owners had an inkling of this intention. The woman of the White household hit on the idea of keeping the couple's baby with her each night so that the young mother would surely not run. (As an aside, the interpersonal relationships of slavery revealed in this nightly caregiving—or abduction—are truly strange to ponder.) Parker learned of the couple's quandary and decided that he would help them. If they could be ready to go, he would simply steal the baby back and they would all cross the river together. The baby's mother, who served as a maid in the home, gave him detailed descriptions of the interior of the big house. Parker crept in and found things as she said; he had difficulty seeing a baby but correctly guessed that it was beside the sleeping woman. He grabbed the child but at the last second a candlestick and two pistols clattered to the floor from a wobbly stool, and the operation became a wild chase. Amazingly, Parker's group eluded the sleepy, but very angry, couple. As far as he knew, the bundle he clutched football-like during his run grew up in Canada.

Over time, John Parker went on to be one of Ripley's most accomplished citizens. Responsibilities kept him in Ripley during the Civil War, but he organized other free Blacks for service, his own sons being too young. Rankin was not as wealthy as the McCagues, but he was very comfortable, as his riverfront home of solid brick reveals. He was a good businessman and a creative ironworker. Just as he had in Mobile, he saw how to do things better and created various new products. He is one of small handful of African Americans who applied for and received patents during the nineteenth

John Parker built this comfortable riverfront home in 1853. *John Parker House*.

century. One of his patents was for a portable tobacco press that became a staple for generations of tobacco growers. Another was for a horse-drawn soil pulverizer, a cousin to a tiller. Besides these new inventions, he produced an array of everyday items; a few fine Ripley homes still sport his intricate wrought-iron fencing.

When not working, Parker relaxed in his house next to the foundry surrounded by books and song. He educated all his children. Two of his sons, one of whom went on to law school, graduated from Oberlin. The Parker daughters studied music. Daughter Hortense is celebrated today for being the first African American to attend, and graduate from, Mount Holyoke. His offspring, the sons and daughters of a once mistreated and scared fugitive slave, melded into college-educated elites of the Black middle class in cities like St. Louis and Chicago.

Through it all, John Parker, the mixed-race man with a large bounty on his head, retained habits from his Underground Railroad days. Parker always walked down the middle of Ripley's streets, shunning all sidewalks, a remnant of the days when a bounty hunter or angry Kentuckian might be lurking in one of Ripley's narrow alleys. He was not going to allow anyone

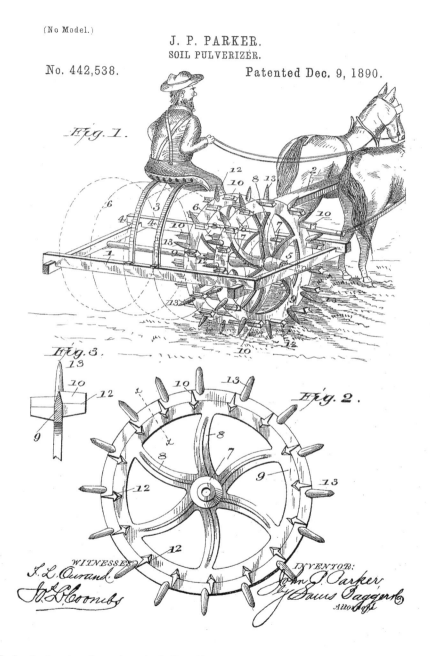

(No Model.)

J. P. PARKER.
SOIL PULVERIZER.

No. 442,538.

Patented Dec. 9, 1890.

Parker had various inventions, including this one patented in 1890. *U.S. Patent Office.*

Hortense Parker was the first African American at Mount Holyoke; husband Marcus Gilliam was a St. Louis school administrator. *Mount Holyoke College Archives and Special Collections.*

to jump out at him. Ripley kids who grew up later in that century thought the old man who always walked in the street was kind of odd. It is doubtful that his appearance actually was odd, but we will never know. In spite of his prosperity and the fashions of the day, John Parker refused to be photographed. There are no known images of Parker or of his wife, Miranda. No stranger, from any alley or anywhere else, was going to see the face of John Parker.

The twentieth century, and now the twenty-first, has not been kind to Ripley's economics. Its river commerce is completely gone. Boatyards, warehouses, slaughterhouses and docks have disappeared, but otherwise the town is strangely unchanged. Its once prosperous and still well-kept Victorian homes stand at attention along Front Street, confronting the river and Kentucky beyond with dignity and gingerbread intact. These were the homes of brave men and women who challenged slavery, opening their doors to freedom seekers many, many nights of the year. Above them, high on the hill, is the home of Reverend Rankin, the revered leader of all. This proud little house, resolutely clinging to the hill's crest, remains our country's best symbol of the Underground Railroad.

Chapter 8

LEGACY OF OHIO'S UNDERGROUND RAILROAD

After the horrible rupture of the Civil War and the difficulties of Reconstruction, Ohio was ready to move on. Written evidence of the Underground Railroad decades before had long ago been burned; descendants were not likely to find relevant documents when their elders died off. There was hearsay only, and a lot of that was disregarded and forgotten. Siebert, who lived until 1961, seemed to be the only person inquiring about the Underground Railroad; most descendants did not ask. Jim Crow tinged even the northern states, and the past noble effort to achieve rights for African Americans was not much talked about—the Underground Railroad finally *did* go underground. Unless you lived in your forebears' grand home with a secret room, and most people did not, you had no idea of their compassion toward freedom seekers. There are people of my generation only dimly aware that their hometown was once a powerhouse of the Underground Railroad—if they know about its role at all. But remnants of the Underground Railroad are all around. That does not just mean some extra cellar doors here and there or old Black settlements, now in decay. The evidence is right in the citizenry.

There is a powerful reminder of Ohio's Underground Railroad in its people, many of whom either came to the state because of the phenomenon or had been shaped by it. These are people of both the White and Black races. Some of the latter had gone to Canada, but a portion gradually filtered back into the United States. As in any migration effort, it is the best and the brightest who accomplish it. A talented Black population came north because of the Underground Railroad. Among Whites, many children were affected by the egalitarian attitudes of their ancestors; some of these families would not have been in Ohio had it not been for its antislavery laws.

One of the state's most accomplished Black families were the Pattersons of Greenfield. Born to slavery in 1833 Virginia, the mixed-race Charles Richard Patterson escaped to the important Underground Railroad town shortly before the Civil War. There he married Josephine Utz, a White woman, and by 1871 he was co-owner of a successful carriage-making business. His youngest son, Frederick, born that year, was named for the great abolitionist Frederick Douglass. After graduating from Greenfield High School, Frederick went on to Ohio State, where he became something of a Big Man on Campus: member of a literary society, business manager of the student newspaper *The Lantern* and elected president of his class. He also played on the football team. His football activity consisted primarily of warming the bench; regardless, he is regarded as Ohio State's first African American player.

Frederick became a teacher but returned to Greenfield when his father's health failed. His father had previously bought out the former partner, so the Pattersons were in full control of their business. Frederick arrived with the insight that times were changing and quickly retooled the workshop for automobile manufacture. He is said to have produced a high-quality car, much like a Model T, thus becoming yet another first: the first African American person to own and operate a car manufacturing plant. Patterson's car may have rivaled Ford's, but he could not compete with Ford's genius in assembly line efficiency. Seeing the problem and having trouble getting credit at local banks, Frederick guided the company into the niche market of buses, especially school buses. The Greenfield Bus Body Company was highly regarded until the Depression caused it to fail. By then, Frederick Patterson was firmly established in Republican politics and in the National Negro Business League. Patterson talent would not have been in Ohio had his father not fled slavery for the state.[110]

The integration of baseball also links to the Underground Railroad in Ohio. You may think this refers to Jackie Robinson, but before him was Moses Fleetwood Walker of Mount Pleasant, a vibrant antislavery community of Quakers and free Blacks in eastern Ohio.[111] The well-educated Moses Walker Sr. and his wife, Caroline, were both mixed-race individuals born free in Pennsylvania and Ohio, respectively. At the time of Moses's 1856 birth, they were assisting fugitives like others in the town and presumably continued the service after moving to Steubenville when young Moses was

Right: Frederick Patterson broke barriers at OSU: class president, *The Lantern* staff, a literary society and the 1891 football team. *The Ohio State University Archives.*

Below: Frederick Patterson manufactured automobiles and buses. His father, Charles, fled slavery and started a carriage business in Greenfield. *Historical Society of Greenfield, Ohio.*

three. There his father became one of Ohio's first Black physicians and also served as a Methodist Episcopal minister. Young Moses played ball games with other kids on the dirt streets of Steubenville; later, he was sent to study at Oberlin, where he excelled in the classroom but found he enjoyed the ball field even more. Oberlin had been fielding a baseball team as far back as the Civil War, with prior integration, so Walker was no novelty. What was new was intercollegiate play, which showcased his skills to a wider audience. Players at the University of Michigan were so impressed that they persuaded Walker to transfer to their larger school. He was pleased that classes in law were available to him there, but as before, classroom work did not hinder his baseball accomplishments. This led to his brief career with the Toledo Blue Stockings in the early days of professional baseball.[112]

Jackie Robinson, of course, later eclipsed Walker in importance and achievement. He had no known connection to Ohio or the Underground Railroad, but the Dodger executive who signed him, Branch Wesley Rickey, did. Rickey grew up outside Portsmouth, on a farm within hailing distance of the both the Ohio and Scioto Rivers. Rickey often told the story of Charles Thomas, an African American player on Ohio Wesleyan's team that Rickey coached in 1904, early in his career. In Rickey's telling, the treatment Thomas suffered and their shared frustrations with it are what drove Rickey to push for modern baseball integration.[113] Rickey neglected to say that his family roots near Portsmouth reveal deep antislavery ties. Rickey's great-grandparents had come to the area from the Northeast in 1817, floating down the Ohio like other early settlers. The family flourished, and everything about them screams antislavery. That first settler was a Baptist minister; later generations of Rickeys aligned themselves with the branch of that church associated with progressivism and antislavery work. They were early staunch Republicans, in that day a marker for opposition to slavery. Fugitive movement flocked up the Scioto River from Portsmouth, a rough town hosting more rascals and slave catchers than Republicans. Scioto County was not a place one could stay neutral on slavery; everyday action forced residents to take a side. There is little doubt what side

Moses Fleetwood Walker was early baseball's first person of color. His parents were active in the Underground Railroad. *National Baseball Hall of Fame and Museum.*

The person here with links to Ohio's Underground Railroad is Branch Rickey, the Dodger executive who signed Jackie Robinson. *Author's collection.*

the Rickeys were on. Branch's uncle, born in February 1861, was given the name Lincoln—by parents clearly overjoyed by the upcoming inauguration. Another uncle was sent to study at Granville Academy, which had a strong abolitionist heritage. What direct assistance this large family offered to fugitives passing through Scioto County is not known, but Underground Railroad activity has been verified in a Kansas branch of their family tree.[114]

It would be interesting to know if any of these baseball men had occasion to attend a game in Zanesville. If so, they were likely in Gant Park, named for Nelson T. Gant; after 1939, its amenities included a modern stadium. The imposing structure, still in use, does not just offer concrete stadium tiers—it is concrete evidence of Ohio's Underground Railroad past. Gant came to the area as a recently freed slave in about 1845, after which he saved money to buy his wife, Anna Marie, out of slavery—and hid fugitives. Successful in both endeavors, Gant was an excellent businessman who eventually owned a large farm, a salt lick and a coal mine. A quiet, thoughtful man, he sent his children to Oberlin College. Gant had received his freedom upon the death of his Virginia owner; upon Gant's 1905 death, he bequeathed acreage to the town for a public park, later to include the popular ball field.[115] Not surprisingly, it is on the western side—the Putnam side—of the Licking River.

Writer Langston Hughes made important breakthroughs not in sport but in literature, extolled as the leader of the Harlem Renaissance of the 1930s. He had a peripatetic upbringing, with only his high school years spent in Ohio. Because his parents had divorced, young Langston was not close to his father. His mother was the daughter of Charles Henry Langston, who had died well before Langston's birth. Regardless, this very important Langston family bestowed on the young poet an interesting heritage as well as his distinctive first name.

Harlem Renaissance poet Langston Hughes descends from the Langston family, prominent Black abolitionists in Ohio. *Library of Congress.*

Charles Langston was born in 1817, the son of a Virginia plantation owner. This owner was a benevolent one who openly claimed his mixed-race sons with his common-law wife, Lucy Langston, who was of Native American and Black heritage. Even so, the boys used their mother's name of Langston and not the name of their father, Ralph Quarles. When Charles was a teen, both his parents died, but the father left a generous inheritance. To live safely, all the Langston boys headed to Ohio with their eldest brother, Gideon. They became well educated, Charles being the first person of color to study at Oberlin. There he met and married Mary Patterson, also biracial and one of its first female students. Langston Hughes was their grandson through daughter Carrie, although grandmother Mary Langston primarily raised him. It was only after her death that Carrie took Langston and moved to Ohio from St. Louis. He began writing and publishing short works while editing his Cleveland school newspaper; then it was on to Columbia.

The Langston brothers were giants of the antislavery movement and the Underground Railroad. At Oberlin, Charles was one of the students charged in the Oberlin-Wellington rescue, the incident in which their classmate John Price was caught and put on a train by slave catchers; a group of students and professors responded by stealing him back. Once Price was safely in Canada, the rest of Oberlin group, Charles included, served several months in jail for their good deed. Charles eventually went to Kansas. His younger brother John Mercer Langston was a famous abolitionist on the scale of Frederick Douglass, a colleague and eventual rival. Active in politics in Ohio and later Virginia, Langston was elected to the U.S. House from the latter state in a contentious 1890 election. He is credited as the first Black man to represent Virginia; in reality, he and many of his political allies were as White as they were Black.[116]

A theme may be apparent in these sketches: the status of the mixed-race. Many of the important Black operatives in the Underground Railroad were mixed-race. The same can generally be said of many of the people of color who relocated to Ohio before the Civil War. An inordinate number of people described in these pages were termed "mulattoes" in those days; in addition to the Pattersons and the Langstons, we find the Woodsons, John Parker, Elijah Anderson and many more. The pattern is so consistent that it becomes the elephant in the room if one does not address it. Why are so many of these Underground Railroad personalities mixed-race? Why did so many mixed-race people come to Ohio?

The answer lies back in the South and in the attitudes of the day. Lighter-skinned people were favored and selected for the best jobs that slavery offered. They were house servants or trained for skill-based jobs. Women became cooks and seamstresses; men mastered work as barbers, blacksmiths, candlemakers, cobblers, coopers, tanners, plasterers, masons, sawyers, carpenters or whatever else the nineteenth century called for.[117] Reading was not uncommon among this crowd, as was rudimentary math.[118] White owners seemed to think that these workers were more able than the darker-skinned, who were mostly relegated to the fields, but this was a self-fulfilling prophecy. These individuals were able because they were allowed to be able.

John Parker, who was exactly right about a great many things, had a sadly skewed explanation for his brilliance. He accepted the dictum of the day that his "White side" made him smart. The real answer is more nuanced. The mixed-race group didn't just learn their trades; their work moved them into the White world. They listened in the big house, always a font of knowledge. They worked with White tradesmen, and they served White customers. Some had travel privileges and knew the lay of the land, including a sense of geography far beyond. Experiences with Whites could naturally lead to reading; if a White playmate liked to play school, then books and letters were the play toys. The outcome of all this interaction is that lighter-skinned Blacks learned to understand and navigate the White world much better than did their cohorts in the fields.

Some enslaved tradespeople were in a position to purchase themselves because they could earn and save extra wages if their output was high. But if they chose the quicker method of running away instead, they were well prepared to do that, too. Women were less likely to independently find their way to freedom than men, but there some who did. Elizabeth Keckley, Mary Todd Lincoln's dressmaker and close friend, began life enslaved, the mixed-race daughter of her owner. With sewing skill and business acumen, she managed to buy her freedom, while also learning to read and write and deal with Washington society. Similarly, Kittie Doram fled her Kentucky birthplace at the age of twelve with thirty-six cents in her pocket. Over time, she established herself in business as a seamstress, reaching financial security while serving Cincinnati's Underground Railroad.[119]

Linked to their skills and general favoritism, those with light coloring were usually worth more if sold. This led to a diabolical situation on some plantations where White owners saw themselves as obliged to father offspring with slave women because it was in their economic self-interest to do so. But the intended payoff did not always work out as planned. Some of these men developed a paternal fondness for their offspring, particularly their sons, so that a number of the boys were trained for a useful career and then freed. And because of local laws, it was best for them to head north. The end result of these factors is that many mixed-race people came to Ohio during slavery. Among Ohio's settlements of color, there were even a few specifically meant for "mulattoes." Longtown, in western Ohio, welcomed residents who looked nearly White.[120] They looked that way because they were mostly White; nonetheless, nineteenth-century laws on race required that they be defined otherwise.

Returning to an actual person and not the load of DNA carried into Ohio, another honored Ohio writer of color is Paul Laurence Dunbar. His parents had both been enslaved in Kentucky; his father managed to extricate himself early in the Civil War and promptly signed on with the "colored units" forming in Massachusetts. His path must have taken him through Ohio and the barely secret Underground Railroad of that decade. He settled in Dayton after the war, where his son Paul honed his writing skills at Dayton's Central High School.[121] A classmate and good friend of this honor student was Orville Wright; elder brother Wilbur became an equally close pal. The Wrights' embrace of the only African American person in their school is reminiscent of earlier activity in the Wright family. Their father was a bishop of the Church of the Brethren, a denomination with a strong antislavery stance. The Wright boys' parents came from families originating

Writer Paul Laurence Dunbar (*top left*) and Orville Wright (*three to his right*) were friends at Dayton's Central High. Both link to the Underground Railroad. *Wright State University Libraries' Special Collections and Archives.*

in the East but had met at the small college of Hartville in Indiana. Their mother, Susan, was sent there partly to foster the unusual math talent she exhibited. Painfully shy, she was most comfortable privately tinkering; in her adult years, she often made handy kitchen devices for herself and toys for her children. Her husband had the more expansive personality. His church work took the family to several towns in eastern Indiana in the 1850s, all of them trod through by freedom seekers. There is little doubt that the deeply religious Wright couple had supported the Underground Railroad.[122]

Another venerated White American with unsung ties to the Underground Railroad is Clark Gable. Gable was born in southeast Ohio, although Pennsylvania also claims him as progeny. His Pennsylvania ancestors operated several different businesses for many years, including hotels in Meadville, of Crawford County. Their earliest was Crawford House; other buildings and name changes also link them to the Barton Hotel and Gable Hotel. Crawford County borders the Ohio state line and is yet another place where the famed John Brown resided, operating a tannery and an Underground Railroad station serving routes that connected both states. Important rail lines passing through Meadville kept hotels busy; it seems that Underground traffic was plentiful as well. Around 1850, Clark Gable's grandfather Charles joined Charles's elder brother John in managing Crawford House. The Gable family quietly hosted fugitives in some of their rooms.[123]

Discovery of oil in Pennsylvania changed the business focus of the next generation of Gables, who launched into oil and mineral extraction. Clark Gable's father, William, relocated to Harrison County, Ohio, where he was contracted to drill a well near the small town of Hopedale. Son Clark was born in the county seat of Cadiz in 1901, but his mother's illness and early death required that he be nurtured by relatives in Pennsylvania during his infancy. When young Clark was a toddler, his father remarried and brought him back to Hopedale, which was much more than an oil and coal town. Not unlike nearby Mount Pleasant, Hopedale had once been a hive of antislavery thought and action. Hopedale Normal School, established by the town's founding family in the 1850s, provided the first coeducational college education in eastern Ohio. Horace Mann taught there for a time; George

These *Gone with the Wind* actors were good friends. Ohioan Clark Gable had progressive views and ancestors in the Underground Railroad. *Author's collection.*

Armstrong Custer was one of its early graduates. The school flourished for a few decades and was even renamed a college, but those days were long past by the time of Clark Gable's childhood. He attended elementary school in one of its old buildings; otherwise, the college had faded away. What remained, however, was a progressive, welcoming attitude in Hopedale, where Gable spent a happy childhood.[124] He enjoyed literature classes as well as theater, likely seeing silent films in an opera house in Cadiz. He would have bought his ticket from a Mr. Walker; the popular town theater was owned and managed by the respected Walker brothers, Moses Fleetwood and Weldy.[125]

In Gable's most famous movie, *Gone with the Wind*, the delightful scenes he played with Hattie McDaniel are an unexpected treat. His Captain Rhett Butler and her "Mammy" liked and respected each other. Little acting was required because this relationship mirrored real life exactly; the two became good friends on set. Gable was incensed when he learned that McDaniel was prohibited from attending the movie's 1939 premiere in Atlanta. He planned to stay away himself until she convinced him to go. He had already made enlightened contributions to the movie. When shooting was set to begin on a California set, Gable learned that separate restroom facilities had inexplicably been set up for the many Black and White extras the film required. He threatened to walk from the role unless this was changed, and it was—quickly.[126] Famous movie star (and later World War II aerial combatant) Clark Gable was very much a product of his antislavery forebears.

These are but a few accomplished Ohioans, people of talent and integrity, who were shaped by the state's antislavery past. The benefits were not just Ohio's—they took those talents and attitudes far beyond state lines and elevated the entire country. In and out of the state, the Underground Railroad is finally being rediscovered and celebrated. But in Ohio, it was there all along, part of the fabric of the state. It remains beneficial to all.

NOTES

Introduction

1. The term "Underground Railroad" is generally understood to mean any system of assistance to fugitive slaves moving north toward Canada. This book will use the term "Underground Railroad" for the entirety of that effort, including the early decades before the term was in use.

Chapter 1

2. Chris Hewitson, "The Lion Salt Works, Northwich: A Legacy of the Cheshire Salt Industry," *Industrial Archeology Review* 39, no.1 (May 2017): 62–63; John A. Jakle, "Salt on the Ohio Valley Frontier, 1770–1820," *Annals of the Association of American Geographers* 59, no. 4 (December 1969): 694–95.

3. The Addison White story has been described by others. Some recommended sources: Baxter, "History of Champaign County, Goshen Township," 585–620; Prince, "Rescue Case of 1857," 292–309; Watts, "History of the Underground Railroad in Mechanicsburg," 209–54; Saxbe, "Questions of Supremacy," 16–23; and Dohron Wilson Scrapbooks, *Addison White, Amanda White, William T. White and Their Descendants* and *The Underground Railroad Scrapbook*. This chapter's narrative is based on these and other research materials but assumes personal thoughts and motivations.

4. Federal Writers' Project, *Slave Narratives: A Folk History of Slavery in the United States from Interviews with Former Slaves*, vol. 7 (Washington, D.C., 1941).

5. Jedediah Hyde II, 1738–1822.

6. Udney Hay, 1739–1806.

7. Gara, *Liberty Line*, 127.

8. Many of Frederick Douglass's papers from his Rochester years were destroyed in a fire. However, the Dohron Wilson Scrapbooks contain an obscure printed reference to this visit; an article clipping (source unclear) donated by a descendant of Charles Taylor quotes Douglass: "[F]etching [Addison] from Urbana to lecture here." The incident is also in the family lore of White's living descendants.

9. This information is from descendants of White; U.S. Army records confirm that White was "sick" and hospitalized March–July 1864. Civil War Service Records—Union—Colored Troops 54th MA Infantry, National Archives, https://www.fold3.com/image/260477190.

10. Old Settlers Reunion Association, *Lett Families Settlement History & Geneaology*, accessed January 1, 2022, https://www.osra1977.org/lett-settlement-history; Sandra W. Perot, "The Dairymaid and the Prince: Race, Memory, and the Story of Benjamin Banneker's Grandmother," *Slavery & Abolition* 38, no. 3 (2017): 445–58.

11. Dohron Wilson Scrapbooks.

12. Judge Evan P. Middleton, *History of Champaign County, Ohio…* (Indianapolis, IN: B.F. Bowen, 1917), 471, https://archive.org/stream/historyofchampai02midd/historyofchampai02midd_djvu.txt.

13. U.S. Federal Census, 1870 and 1880.

Chapter 2

14. This period of Ohio history is well described in McCullough, *Pioneers*.

15. Jakle, "Salt on the Ohio Valley Frontier," 687–709.

16. Calculated from Valley Forge Legacy: The Muster Roll Project, last modified September 24, 2019, https://valleyforgemusterroll.org.

17. Robert A. Selig, "The Revolution's Black Soldiers," American Revolution, accessed June 5, 2021, https://www.americanrevolution.org/blk.php.

18. Ronald Shannon, *Profiles in Ohio History: A Legacy of African American Achievement* (N.p.: iUniverse, 2008), https://www.washogs.org/aa_ancestors/afam-ancestors.html.

19. Find a Grave, "Richard Stanhope," accessed February 3, 2021, https://www.findagrave.com/memorial/7584460/richard-stanhope.
20. Gara, *Liberty Line*, 43; Lucas, *History of Blacks in Kentucky*, 120.
21. Sheeler, "Struggle of the Negro," 210.
22. Gara, *Liberty Line*, 20, 65.
23. "Quakers First Settle in Ohio 1800 to 1805," from *Historic Atlas of Ohio Yearly Meeting*, 12–13, accessed November 20, 2021, https://www.quaker-chronicle.info/pdfs/pp12-13.pdf.

Chapter 3

24. Griffler, *Front Line of Freedom*, 93; Siebert, *Ohio's Network of the Underground Railroad*, Section II (draft), Wilbur H. Siebert Underground Railroad Collection, Ohio History Connection, https://www.ohiomemory.org/digital/collection/siebert/id/904/rec/2.
25. Fox, "Searching for Poke Patch."
26. Griffler thoroughly covers this area.
27. "The Storyteller," *Columbus Monthly*, July 1, 2010, https://amp.columbusmonthly.com/amp/22783751007; Daniel Strawter to Wilbur Siebert, undated, https://ohiomemory.org/digital/collection/siebert/id/7776/rec/1.
28. Alvin Adams, "'Colored' Underground Railroad Workers in Southeastern Ohio," in *Underground Railroad Workers in Southeastern Ohio*, accessed October 20, 2021, https://henryburke1010.tripod.com/id75.html.
29. Griffler, *Front Line of Freedom*, 12–14.
30. Van Horne–Lane, *Safe Houses and the Underground Railroad*, 58.
31. Calarco, *Search for the Underground Railroad*, 40–41; Griffler, *Front Line of Freedom*, 32–35.
32. Multiple Woodson descendants unknown to one another share a similar understanding of their heritage. Annette Gordon-Reed, a prominent scholar of the Jefferson-Hemings relationship and their proven offspring, agrees that strong evidence links the Woodsons of Ohio to Sally Hemings. However, this link does not extend to proof of Jefferson's paternity in *this* family line, which Gordon-Reed doubts, or that Sally's child born in 1790 is Thomas Woodson. Her conclusion is that there is indeed a connection between the Woodson family and individual(s) at Monticello, but it is unclear what the connection is. *Thomas Jefferson and Sally Hemings: An American Controversy* (Charlottesville: University of Virginia Press, 1998), 67–77.

33. R.C. Hall, "Quakers in Southern Ohio," *Herald-Advisor* (Huntington, WV), July 17, 1938, in the *Lawrence Register*, https://lawrencecountyohio.com/stories/quakers-in-southern-ohio.

34. Henson, *Autobiography of Josiah Henson*. Henson is assumed to have inspired Harriet Beecher Stowe's character Uncle Tom, but this association gives him too little credit.

35. Edward O'Connor Purtee, "The Underground Railroad from Southwest Ohio to Lake Erie," diss., Ohio State University, 1932, 65, https://www.ohiomemory.org/digital/collection/siebert/id/5810/rec/1.

36. Roy E. Finkenbine, "The Native Americans Who Assisted the Underground Railroad," History News Network, accessed March 4, 2022, https://historynewsnetwork.org/article/173041; [King Family Genealogy], accessed April 3, 2021, http://sites.rootsweb.com/~ohfulton/UNDERGROUNDRAILROADOFNWOHIO.htm; Diane Miller, "Wyandot, Shawnee, and African American Resistance to Slavery in Ohio and Kansas" (diss., University of Nebraska–Lincoln, 2019), https://digitalcommons.unl.edu/historydiss/94.

Chapter 4

37. Van Horne–Lane, *Safe Houses and the Underground Railroad*, 55.

38. Beckert, *Empire of Cotton*, 104.

39. U.S. Census Bureau, "Statistics of the United States," *1850 Census: Compendium of the Seventh Census*, 82. https://www2.census.gov/library/publications/decennial/1850/1850c/1850c-04.pdf.

40. Bogert, "Sold for My Account," 6.

41. Ibid., 8.

42. Emily Bingham, *My Old Kentucky Home: The Astonishing Life and Reckoning of an Iconic American Song* (New York: Knopf, 2022), xi. Stephen Foster's original 1853 lyrics, long ago scrubbed, clearly describe slaves relocated into sugarcane fields expressing nostalgia for their homeland.

43. Gara, *Liberty Line*, 63; Litwack, *North of Slavery*, 68–72.

44. Gara, *Liberty Line*, 23–24; Hagedorn, *Beyond the River*, 38.

45. Wolf, "Margaret Garner," 417–40.

Chapter 5

46. Sprague, *His Promised Land*, 72, 138–39.
47. "Elijah Anderson, Underground Railroad Conductor."
48. "Some Recollections of the Underground Railroad in Belmont County, Ohio," accessed October 3, 2021, http://genealogytrails.com/ohio/belmont/undergroundrailroad.html; Van Horne–Lane, *Safe Houses and the Underground Railroad*, 15.
49. Griffler, *Front Line of Freedom*, 59–60; Coffin, *Reminiscences of Levi Coffin*, 305–11, 428–46.
50. Copeland, *Ain't No Harm to Kill the Devil*, 313–20; U.S. Census, 1860.
51. Bradford, *Scenes in the Life of Harriet Tubman*, 27–28+.
52. Historical Marker, "The Ohio River: Ever Changing," https://www.hmdb.org/m.asp?m=16689; W.B. Langbein, *Hydrology and Environmental Aspects of Erie Canal (1817–99)*, Geological Survey Water-Supply Paper 2038, Washington, D.C.: Government Printing Office, 1976.
53. Hagedorn, *Beyond the River*, 12.
54. Lucas, *History of Blacks in Kentucky*, 64.
55. Clio Admin, Nathan Wuertenberg and Kathleen Thompson, "Women of Courage Historical Marker (Aunt Jenny and the Underground Railroad)," Clio: Your Guide to History, October 8, 2020, accessed March 6, 2021, https://theclio.com/tour/1083/2.
56. Gragston, "Narrative of Arnold Gragston."
57. "Employees of the Anti-Slavery League from Pioneer History of Indiana," 216, accessed March 5, 2021, https://www.ohiomemory.org/digital/collection/siebert/id/10794/rec/2.
58. Purtee, "Underground Railroad from Southwest Ohio to Lake Erie," 34.
59. Hagedorn, *Beyond the River*, 135–39, 208–14.
60. Delblanco, *War Before the War*, 110.
61. Bogert, "Sold for My Account," 3–16; Hagedorn, *Beyond the River*, 330.
62. Purtee, "Underground Railroad from Southwest Ohio to Lake Erie," 33.

Chapter 6

63. Calarco, *Search for the Underground Railroad*, 98–99.
64. "Cincinnati: A Guide to the Queen City and Its Neighbors," Writer's Program, 1943, https://ohiomemory.org/digital/collection/siebert/id/6481/rec/3.

65. Wilbur H. Siebert, *Mysteries of Ohio's Underground Railroad*, Section II (draft), 8, https://ohiomemory.org/digital/collection/siebert/id/1175/rec/2.

66. Paul D. Quick, "Slaves Once Passed through Here," *Columbus Citizen*, May 26, 1947, https://www.ohiomemory.org/digital/collection/siebert/id/6461/rec/1.

67. Gara, *Liberty Line*, 180.

68. Norris F. Schneider, "Zanesville Rioters Attacked Putnam Conductors of the Underground Railroad," *Zanesville News*, October 17, 1943, https://www.ohiomemory.org/digital/collection/siebert/id/6686/rec/1.

69. YouTube, "Home Tour," accessed March 30, 2022, https://www.youtube.com/watch?v=sJjftkK9DIk.

70. Many sources discuss Siebert, including Calarco, *Search for the Underground Railroad*, 27–34; Griffler, *Front Line of Freedom*, 2–4, 8–9; and Gara, *Liberty Line*, 190–92.

71. Schulz, "Derailed," 66–73.

72. Foner, *Gateway to Freedom*, 10. For Ripley's calculation, see chapter 7.

73. Fairchild, "Underground Railroad," 105.

74. Still, *Underground Railroad*, v.

75. Henry T. Buttersworth to Wilbur Siebert [on behalf of his wife], June 9, 1892, 2, https://ohiomemory.org/digital/collection/siebert/id/7649/rec/1.

76. Schneider, "Zanesville Rioters Attacked Putnam Conductors," 9.

77. A few Jews of the South owned slaves, although it was counter to their faith.

78. Klinger, "August Bondi"; Bondi, *Autobiography of August Bondi*, 32, 171.

79. Stacie Narlock and Holly Teasdale, "The Underground Railroad: Little Known Jewish Connections," *Michigan Jewish History* 45 (2005): 51–57.

80. Kathy Rupert Schulz, "The Vance Migration to the Underground Railroad of Southwestern Ohio," *Official Newsletter of the Vance Family Association* 34, no. 4 (Winter 2018): 69–81.

81. Buttersworth to Wilbur Siebert, 2.

82. Quoted by Siebert in "Underground Railroad," 12, https://www.ohiomemory.org/digital/collection/siebert/id/15979/rec/3.

83. Christopher Densmore, "Quakers and the Underground Railroad: Myths and Realities," accessed February 9, 2022, https://web.tricolib.brynmawr.edu/speccoll/quakersandslavery/commentary/organizations/underground_railroad.pdf.

84. Cathy D. Nelson, e-mail message to author, March 9, 2022. Nelson—a retired history teacher, founder of the Friends of Freedom Society and authority on the Underground Railroad—has promoted the work of the Columbus Metropolitan Quilters. Nonetheless, she shares the view that these creations are based on modern thought, with designs that lacked directional symbolism to nineteenth-century freedom seekers.

85. William W. Keifer to Wilbur Siebert, October 21, 1948, and November 21, 1949, https://ohiomemory.org/digital/collection/siebert/id/4726/rec/1; "Elizabeth Piatt: A Pioneering Woman, West Liberty Historical Society," accessed February 16, 2022, https://www.westlibertyhistory.com/west-liberty-history-stories/elizabeth-piatt-a-pioneering-woman, apparently based on *A Memorial Biography of Benjamin and Elizabeth, His Wife*, written by two granddaughters in 1887.

86. David Pilgrim, "Lawn Jockeys," *Jim Crow Museum of Racist Memorabilia*, Ferris State University, July 2018, https://www.ferris.edu/HTMLS/news/jimcrow/question/2008/july.htm; Kate Larson, Underground Railroad Research Forum, April 20, 2008, https://www.afrigeneas.com/forum-ugrr/index.cgi/md/read/id/1992/sbj/piatt-of-ohio.

87. Coffin, *Reminiscences of Levi Coffin*, 307–9.

88. Hannah W. Blackburn to the U.G.R.R. Circular, April 5, 1893, https://ohiomemory.org/digital/collection/siebert/id/6357/rec/19.

89. Wilbur H. Siebert, *Mysteries of Ohio's Underground Railroad*, Section III (draft), 63–64.

90. Newton Pierce to Wilbur Siebert, February 1, 1893, https://ohiomemory.org/digital/collection/siebert/id/7993/rec/3; Wilbur H. Siebert, *Mysteries of Ohio's Underground Railroad*, Section III (draft), 75.

91. Craft and Craft, *Running a Thousand Miles for Freedom*.

92. Griffler, *Front Line of Freedom*, 51.

93. Calarco, *Search for the Underground Railroad*, 91–92.

94. Purtee, "Underground Railroad from Southwest Ohio to Lake Erie," 16.

95. Woodard, *American Nations*.

96. Purtee, "Underground Railroad from Southwest Ohio to Lake Erie," 14–15.

97. N.B. Sisson to Wilbur Siebert, September 16, 1894. https://www.ohiomemory.org/digital/collection/siebert/id/4128/rec/4.

98. Cris Swetye, "Did Local Historians Research Accurately?," *Salem News*, January 6, 1993, *Yesteryears* [section] 2, no. 16, 8.

Chapter 7

99. This chapter is based largely on two sources: Parker's dictated autobiography, edited by Sprague, and the outstanding research on Ripley and its citizens by Hagedorn.
100. Name is unknown.
101. H.W. Brands, *Heirs of the Founders: The Epic Rivalry of Henry Clay, John Calhoun, and Daniel Webster, the Second Generation of Giants* (New York: Anchor, 2018), 136.
102. Data is from 1846, *History of Brown County, Ohio…* (Chicago: W.H. Beers, 1883), 441.
103. Sheeler, "Struggle of the Negro," 211; Middleton, "Fugitive Slave Crisis in Cincinnati," 23.
104. Coffin, *Reminiscences of Levi Coffin*, title page; Middleton, "Fugitive Slave Crisis in Cincinnati," 20–32; Cooper and Jackson, *Cincinnati's Underground Railroad*, 78.
105. Purtee, "Underground Railroad from Southwest Ohio to Lake Erie," 53.
106. Ron Chernow, *Grant* (New York: Penguin, 2017), 3–18.
107. John Parker House tour guide Dewey Scott; the number may be approximate. John Parker's autobiography confirms that there were multiple shoemakers in Ripley; the 1883 county history lists nine.
108. Sprague, *His Promised Land*, 165.
109. Ohio History Central, "John Rankin," accessed March 6, 2022, https://ohiohistorycentral.org/w/John_Rankin#:~:text=Rankin%20gave%20shelter%20and%20food,her%20book%2C%20Uncle%20Tom's%20Cabin.

Chapter 8

110. National Museum of African American History and Culture, "The Only African American Automobile Company," September 26, 2014, https://nmaahc.si.edu/explore/stories/only-african-american-automobile-company; Zach Shremp, "C.R. Patterson & Sons Company (1893–1939)," Black Past, October 26, 2010, https://www.blackpast.org/african-american-history/c-r-patterson-sons-company-1893-1939; Carmen Collection, "Class President, Football Player, Horton Society Member—and Son of a Former Escaped Slave," Ohio State University, https://carmencollection.osu.edu/

story/class-president-football-player-horton-society-member-and-son-escaped-former-slave.

111. The Society for American Baseball Research believes that William Edward White, presenting himself as White while actually mixed-race, predated Walker in baseball by a few years with a single game appearance. However, Walker is the first baseball player to openly play as Black. Walker's younger brother Weldy also played.

112. Wikipedia, "Moses Fleetwood Walker," last modified March 7, 2022, https://en.wikipedia.org/wiki/Moses_Fleetwood_Walker; John R. Husman, "Moses Fleetwood Walker," Society for American Baseball Research, accessed February 2, 2022, https://sabr.org/bioproj/person/fleet-walker.

113. Thomas occasionally suffered harsh treatment on the road during his baseball years, but his later life was rewarding. After Ohio Wesleyan, he studied dentistry at Ohio State, graduating in 1908. He had a dental career in Albuquerque, New Mexico, that lasted forty years. He and Rickey remained lifelong close friends. Battling Bishops, "OWU Celebrates Courage, Character, and the Life of Charles Thomas," https://battlingbishops.com/news/2021/2/25/GEN_02252021.aspx.

114. Nelson Wiley Evans, *History of Scioto County, Ohio: Together with a Pioneer Record of Southern Ohio* (New York: self-published, 1903), 817–18, 1,114–15; Mary Ann Calvert, Rickey material in Caldwell [Ohio] Public Library Digital Shoebox Project, accessed March 5, 2022, http://www.digitalshoebox.org/digital/collection/caldbooks/id/10273/rec/4.

115. Christine Holmes, "Updates Planned for Stadium that Has Served as Summer Hub for Generations," *Zanesville Times Recorder*, March 7, 2021, https://www.google.com/search?q=times+recorder+gant+stadium&rlz=1C1CHBF_enUS988US988&oq=times+recorder+gant+stadium&aqs=chrome..69i57.6456j0j7&sourceid=chrome&ie=UTF-8; Nelson T. Gant Foundation, accessed April 12, 2022, https://www.nelsontgantfoundation.org.

116. Griffler, *Front Line of Freedom*, 52–53; Calarco, *Search for the Underground Railroad*, 42–45; Wikipedia, "Langston Hughes," last modified March 12, 2022, https://en.wikipedia.org/wiki/Langston_Hughes.

117. Gara, *Liberty Line*, 42–43.

118. Ibid., 159.

119. Griffler, *Front Line of Freedom*, 102.

120. W.E.B. Du Bois, "Long in Darke," *Colored American Magazine* 17, no. 5 (November 1909): 352–55.

121. Wright State Universities, Special Collections & Archives, "Paul Laurence Dunbar: Highlights of A Life," accessed March 15, 2022, https://www.libraries.wright.edu/special/dunbar/biography.php; Poetry Foundation, "Paul Laurence Dunbar," accessed March 15, 2022, https://www.poetryfoundation.org/poets/paul-laurence-dunbar.

122. David McCullough, *The Wright Brothers* (New York: Simon & Schuster, 2015), 10–11, 19–20; Wikipedia, "Wright Brothers," last modified April 4, 2022, https://en.wikipedia.org/wiki/Wright_brothers; Nicholas Patler, "Opening Doors: Building an Underground Railroad Community in Wayne County Indiana," *Traces of Indiana and Midwestern History* 29, no. 2 (Winter 2017): 38+, https://go.gale.com/ps/i.do?id=GALE%7CA488658318&sid=googleScholar&v=2.1&it=r&linkaccess=abs&issn=1040788X&p=AONE&sw=w&userGroupName=nm_p_oweb&isGeoAuthType=true.

123. *History of Crawford County, Pennsylvania…* (Chicago: Warner Beers, 1885), 739–40; "The Underground Railroad's Secret Operations in Crawford County," *Crawford Messenger*, February 28, 2016, http://crawfordpahistory.blogspot.com/2016/02/the-underground-railroads-secret.html.

124. Village of Hopedale, "Our History," accessed February 8, 2022, www.hopedaleohio.com/our-history.

125. Husman, "Moses Fleetwood Walker."

126. Ronald E. Franklin, "Clark Gable Desegregates 'Gone with the Wind' Movie Set," Reel Rundown, March 30, 2022, https://reelrundown.com/film-industry/Clark-Gable-Desegregates-Gone-With-The-Wind-Movie-Set.

SELECTED BIBLIOGRAPHY

General Studies

Beckert, Sven. *Empire of Cotton: A Global History*. New York, Vintage, 2014.

Blight, David W., ed. *Passages to Freedom: The Underground Railroad in History and Memory*. New York: Smithsonian Books, 2004.

Bordewich, Fergus M. *Bound for Canaan: The Epic Story of the Underground Railroad, America's First Civil Rights Movement*. New York: Amistad, 2016.

Delblanco, Andrew. *The War Before the War: Fugitive Slaves and the Struggle for America's Soul from the Revolution to the Civil War*. New York: Penguin, 2018.

Foner, Eric. *Gateway to Freedom: The Hidden History of the Underground Railroad*. New York: Norton, 2015.

Gara, Larry. *The Liberty Line: The Legends of the Underground Railroad*. Lexington: University Press of Kentucky, 1967.

Griffler, Keith P. *Front Line of Freedom: African Americans and the Forging of the Underground Railroad in the Ohio Valley*. Lexington: University Press of Kentucky, 2004.

Hagedorn, Ann. *Beyond the River: The Untold Story of the Heroes of the Underground Railroad*. New York: Simon & Schuster, 2002.

LaRoche, Cheryl Janifer. *Free Black Communities and the Underground Railroad: The Geography of Resistance*. Champaign-Urbana: University of Illinois Press, 2013.

Litwack, Leon F. *North of Slavery: The Negro in the Free States, 1790–1860*. Chicago: University of Chicago Press, 1961.

McCullough, David. *The Pioneers: The Heroic Story of the Settlers Who Brought the American Ideal West*. New York: Simon & Schuster, 2019.

Schulz, Kathryn. "Derailed." *New Yorker* 92, no. 25 (August 22, 2016): 66–73.

Sheeler, J. Reuben. "The Struggle of the Negro in Ohio for Freedom." *Journal of Negro History* 31, no. 2 (April 1946): 208–26.

Siebert, Wilbur H. *The Underground Railroad from Slavery to Freedom*. New York: Macmillan, 1898.

Wilbur H. Siebert Underground Railroad Collection. Ohio History Connection. https://www.ohiomemory.org/digital/collection/siebert.

Woodard, Colin. *American Nations: A History of the Eleven Regional Cultures of North America*. New York: Viking, 2011.

Individual People and Locations of the Underground Railroad Period

Baxter, W.H. "History of Champaign County, Goshen Township." In *History of Champaign County, Ohio: Containing a History of the County; Its Cities, Towns, Etc*…. Chicago: W.H. Beers, 1881. Google Books, https://www.google.com/books/edition/The_History_of_Champaign_County_Ohio/pQzVAAAAMAAJ?hl=en.

Bogert, Pen. "'Sold for My Account': The Early Slave Trade Between Kentucky and the Lower Mississippi Valley." *Ohio Valley History* 2, no. 1 (Spring 2002): 3–16.

Bondi, August Mendel. *Autobiography of August Bondi, 1833–1907*. Galesburg, IL: Wagoner Printing, 1910.

Bradford, Sarah H. *Scenes in the Life of Harriet Tubman*. Auburn, NY: H.J. Moses, 1869. https://docsouth.unc.edu/neh/bradford.bradford.html.

Calarco, Tom. *The Search for the Underground Railroad in South-Central Ohio*. Charleston SC: The History Press, 2018.

Coffin, Levi. *Reminiscences of Levi Coffin: The Reputed President of the Underground Railroad; Being a Brief History of the Labors of a Lifetime in Behalf of the Slave, With Stories of Numerous Fugitives Who Gained Their Freedom Through His Instrumentality and Many Other Incidents*. Cincinnati, OH: Western Tract Society, 1876. Kindle.

Cooper, Richard, and Dr. Eric R. Jackson. *Cincinnati's Underground Railroad*. Charleston SC: Arcadia Publishing, 2014.

Copeland, Jeffrey S. *Ain't No Harm to Kill the Devil: The Life and Legend of John Fairfield, Abolitionist for Hire*. St. Paul, MN: Paragon House, 2014.

Craft, Ellen, and William Craft. *Running a Thousand Miles for Freedom, Or, The Escape of Ellen and William Craft from Slavery*. London: Tweedie, 1860. Google Books, https://www.google.com/books/edition/Running_a_Thousand_Miles_for_Freedom_Or/1mkBAAAAQAAJ?hl=en&gbpv=1&printsec=frontcover.

Dohron Wilson Scrapbooks, Mechanicsburg Public Library, Mechanicsburg, Ohio. *Addison White, Amanda White, William T. White and Their Descendants: A Scrapbook* and *The Underground Railroad Scrapbook: Mechanicsburg, Champaign County, Ohio.*

"Elijah Anderson, Underground Railroad Conductor." In *Encyclopedia of Northern Kentucky* (Lexington: University Press of Kentucky, 2009), accessed August 10, 2021, http://www.historybyperrine.com/tag/elijah-anderson.

Fairchild, James H. "The Underground Railroad." *Western Reserve Historical Society* IV, Tract 87, 1895.

Fox, Wilma. "Searching for Poke Patch." *Lawrence Register*, accessed March 5, 2022, https://lawrencecountyohio.com/stories/african-american/searching-for-poke-patch-african-american-history.

Gragston, Arnold. "Narrative of Arnold Gragston." *Making of African American Identity*, vol. 1, *1500–1865*, National Humanities Center Resources Toolbox, 2007, http://nationalhumanitiescenter.org/pds/maai/community/text7/gragstonwpanarrative.pdf.

Henson, Josiah. *Autobiography of Josiah Henson: Formerly a Slave, Now an Inhabitant of Canada, as Narrated by Himself*. Boston: Phelps, 1849. Google Books, https://www.google.com/books/edition/The_Life_of_Josiah_Henson_Formerly_a_Sla/nAY4AQAAIAAJ?hl=en&gbpv=1&printsec=frontcover.

Klinger, Jerry. "August Bondi: The Abolitionist Jew Who Fought to Free the American Slaves." Jewish-American Society for Historic Preservation, accessed October 3, 2021, http://www.jewish-american-society-for-historic-preservation.org/images/August_Bondi-pdf-2.pdf.

Lucas, Marion B. *A History of Blacks in Kentucky: From Slavery to Segregation, 1760–1891*. Frankfort: Kentucky Historical Society, 2003.

Middleton, Stephen. "The Fugitive Slave Crisis in Cincinnati, 1850–1860: Resistance, Enforcement and Black Refugees." *Journal of Negro History* 72, nos. 1–2 (Winter–Spring 1987): 20-32.

Prince, Benjamin F. "The Rescue Case of 1857." *Ohio Archaeological and Historical Society Publications* 16, no. 3 (July 1907): 292–309.

Purtee, Edward O'Connor. "The Underground Railroad from Southwest Ohio to Lake Erie." PhD diss., Ohio State University, 1932. https://www.ohiomemory.org/digital/collection/siebert/id/5810/rec/1.

Saxbe, William B., Jr. "Questions of Supremacy." *Timeline* 30, no. 2 (April–June 2013): 16–23.

Sprague, Stuart Steely, ed. *His Promised Land: The Autobiography of John P. Parker, Former Slave and Conductor on the Underground Railroad*. New York: Norton, 1996.

Still, William. *The Underground Railroad: Authentic Narratives and First-Hand Accounts*. Edited by Ian Frederick Finseth. Mineola, NY: Dover, 2007.

Taylor, Nikki M. *Frontiers of Freedom: Cincinnati's Black Community, 1802–1868*. Athens: Ohio University Press, 2005.

Van Horne–Lane, Janice. *Safe Houses and the Underground Railroad in East Central Ohio*. Charleston, SC: The History Press, 2010.

Watts, Ralph M. "History of the Underground Railroad in Mechanicsburg." *Ohio History Journal* 43, no. 3 (July 1934): 209–54. Ohio History Connection. https://resources.ohiohistory.org/ohj/browse/displaypages.php?display[]=0043&display[]=209&display[]=254.

Wolf, Cynthia Griffin. "'Margaret Garner': A Cincinnati Story." *Massachusetts Review* 32, no. 3 (Fall 1991): 417–40.

INDEX

A

abolitionist vs. antislavery 70
Adams County, Ohio 53, 112
Adler, Rabbi Liebman 92
African Methodist Episcopals 35, 92
Akron, Ohio 104
Alabama 13, 46, 64, 92, 109
Alexandria, Virginia 76
Alliance, Ohio 99
Alum Creek, Ohio 22, 27
American Revolution 17, 20, 38, 39, 40, 43, 46
Anderson, Elijah 73, 129
Antislavery Bugle (Salem, Ohio) 106
Appalachian Mountains 38, 40, 50, 76, 102
Arkansas 64, 68
Arrowhead Golf Club, Canton 54
Ashtabula, Ohio 74
Atlanta, Georgia 133
Aunt Jenny. *See* Sutton, Edna

B

Bannaka, Prince 32
Banneker, Benjamin 32
Baptists 44, 50, 51, 92, 126
Barrow, Amanda. *See* White, Amanda Barrow
baseball 124, 126, 127
  Brooklyn Dodgers 126
  Oberlin 126
  Ohio Wesleyan 126
  Toledo Blue Stockings 126
  University of Michigan 126
Battle of Combahee Ferry 32
Battle of Fallen Timbers 39
Battle of Fort Wagner 32
Battle of Yorktown, 1781 43
Beasley, Drs. (brothers) 113
Beecher, Harriet. *See* Stowe, Harriet Beecher
Beecher, Lyman 115, 117
Beecher, Reverend William 106
Belmont County, Ohio 55
Belpre, Ohio 76

H

I

ABOUT THE AUTHOR

Kathy Schulz is a retired college librarian. A native Ohioan, she has deep roots in the state and degrees from three of its universities. She lived at two major Underground Railroad junctions and wants Americans to know that the Underground Railroad was mostly in Ohio and mostly above ground—not in tunnels! Kathy and her husband currently live in Santa Fe, New Mexico, where she stays busy with friends, hobbies and grandchildren.

Visit us at
www.historypress.com